The Rise and Fall
of the Plantation South

THE RISE AND FALL
OF THE
PLANTATION
SOUTH

Raimondo Luraghi

NEW VIEWPOINTS

A Division of Franklin Watts

New York | London | 1978

New Viewpoints
A Division of Franklin Watts
730 Fifth Avenue
New York, New York 10019

Library of Congress Cataloging in Publication Data

Luraghi, Raimondo.
The rise and fall of the Plantation South.

Bibliography: p.
Includes index.
1. Southern States—History—Colonial period ca.
1600–1775.   2. Southern States—History—1775–
1865.   3. Plantation life—Southern States—His-
tory.   4. Southern States—Economic conditions.
I. Title.
F212.L8   975   77–15606
ISBN 0–531–05396–2
ISBN 0–531–05606–6 pbk.

Preface

What can a military historian contribute to the study of a cultural history phenomenon such as that of the rise and fall of the seigneurial class? And, furthermore, what does this strange word "seigneurial" mean? Both questions require some discussion.

As I have stated elsewhere, military problems, if studied in a vacuum, do not make much sense. War is the hardest test to which a given society is subjected. Every society meets this challenging strain in a way that is directly linked to its social, moral, ethical—in other words, its cultural—scale of values. Consequently, we could say that any people are led, both politically and militarily, in the way "they deserve" to be; or, less drastically, that any society wages its own peculiar kind of warfare. It was not by chance that the Romans, during the Punic wars, used a wide *levée en masse*, whereas the Carthaginians had to rely mainly on mercenary troops, or even that modern, industrial countries make use of technological warfare, which was pushed by Hitler to the very point of "industrializing death."

When I first became involved in the fascinating field of study (and that was twenty years ago) of the American Civil

5

War, I began to study closely both social and cultural structures in nineteenth-century America. It was like traveling to what really amounted to (and still amounts to in the mind of many a European) a New World or, as Sir Walter Ralegh would have put it, "the Newe Worlde." An immense landscape began to evolve before my eyes as I plunged more and more deeply into records and books on both sides of the Atlantic, or as I ploughed through scores of old sleepy villages, down unending highways and byways, and across wide rivers and mountain ranges. It was indeed one of those adventures that is the most wonderful reward in the sometimes hard destiny of being a historian.

The results of my twenty-year-long research are in other books. Here, I am trying only to condense what seems to me the underlying meaning of a gigantic struggle for a continent that lasted almost five centuries (and may not yet be over). The great colonizing wave came from a European world where the bourgeois class (which was the true driving power of the wave) still had to share its leadership with old-fashioned, truly medieval institutions such as absolute monarchies, universal churches, and military nobilities. All this, transplanted to the Americas, produced a remarkably original civilization, one we have almost lost the flavor of.

Certainly this society did have dark and in some cases ghastly sides; however, what other civilization might feel itself innocent enough to be entitled to stone-throwing? In any case, it certainly succeeded to a remarkable degree in creating a "culture" of its own, a culture which, if studied carefully and "with love," is still among the richest and most fascinating of the world. *Such* was the society that fought the Civil War—and died game, bequeathing to posterity a cultural heritage worthy of understanding.

Here is the stumbling block: it is extremely difficult to approach a dead world with its own viewpoint, not with ours. And here is where I have strong exceptions to take to the otherwise interesting work of the so-called "Cliometricians," or is it not better to call them simply "econometricians"? (Is not Clio, the muse of history, too awesome to be so easily disturbed?)

Let me state clearly what I mean. I have, of course, nothing against econometrics, which, indeed, I consider a most useful tool for historical research. All the honors given to distinguished colleagues for discovering such a new tool are well deserved. For some of them, such as Bob Fogel or Stan Engerman, I have not only respect, but even friendship. However, the major "sin" of the econometricians is, in my mind, that having discovered what amounts simply to a new (or not so new) heuristic tool, they proceed to discard every other tool, and sometimes jump to hasty, unwarranted conclusions without bothering to do complete historical research.

Econometrics must be handled very carefully. (By itself, it is among the most genuine products of our technological civilization, not much different from atomic missiles or thermonuclear bombs.) This means that, when applying this tool to old-fashioned civilizations, one has to be exceptionally prudent, otherwise, such a sophisticated and awesome tool might "kill" outright our poor old men, sons of a totally different era, instead of helping us to understand them. In other words, it is like trying to understand the way pioneers crossed the American continent by flying over it in a jet. Any historic era, any dead society, must be understood, as Italian Renaissance men have said, *juxta propria principia* and, I would strongly add, by using as much as possible the society's own tools for an understanding, not ours. Consequently, in a sense, many econometricians bring to my mind that positivist surgeon who used to say that the soul simply did not exist, since, having cut to pieces several scores of human bodies, he never happened to find one. And yet, he was a most prominent scientist in his own era.

So, the most we will say to our econometricians is: "We warmly thank you for this new weapon you have added to the arsenal of history; we certainly shall ask your help in handling it (albeit carefully)"—and this is all. As far as talk of a "new history" is concerned, we have only to say, *nec sutor ultra crepidam.*

One word on my use of the term "seigneurial." It is French, of course. It comes from old French Canada (with influences from French Louisiana). However, it is, in my mind, the only correct term to be applied to that protean and wonderful class who built a civilization in America. They defended it fiercely against heavy odds, fighting Dutch, British, and Yankees, and fell, burying themselves under its debris. If you dare to enter such a "valley of shadows," the fallen civilization still looks imposing, and still speaks to whoever cares to listen. To call them "planters" could be unfair to French "seigneurs," Latin-American "haciendados," or Brazilian "senhores de en-genho." The word "planter" is, to my mind, a term limited too much to economic and social patterns. To call them a "feudal class," could be wrong, as they lacked some of the essential characteristics of feudalism. However, sometimes they preserved these characteristics in an embryonic and concealed way, like a third eye, or the tail in human beings. The fact is, that the Southern seigneurial class was a genuine product of the Americas, and is not to be found elsewhere. In space, as in time, its scope was limited.

My approach enabled me to see the basic morphologic similarities between societies as far apart as New France, the Old South, Brazil, and the Caribbean islands; and this, of course, took me on a journey not only through almost countless archives and libraries, but also through places as different as the banks of the chilling and imposing St. Lawrence, the sunny cotton fields of the Old South, and the torrid shores of Latin America. It was an experience never to be forgotten; indeed, the experience of a lifetime.

Thus, what I am presenting here to my kind readers is not in itself the result of a single piece of research, but the product of meditations that have spanned a lifetime, condensed in only a few pages. Truly, on this subject I might well have written a score of volumes; however, they would hardly have been read as, hopefully, this small one will be. They certainly would have looked much too grim and forbidding to achieve the goal I want more than any other: *viz.*, driving people to challenge my views—and by this, to increase and deepen the research in this field. Human life is limited, so I would like to see people going ahead to further researching horizons that I may scarcely hope to reach in what time is still left to me in this world.

I have reduced footnotes to a minimum, otherwise they would have been far longer than the book itself; however, I beg the readers to believe that there is not a single line in this book that is not founded upon years of research and meditation, and on hundreds (actually, thousands) of records.

In my many years in the historical profession I have met scores of wonderful people, from whom I have received the most cordial, friendly, and open collaboration, and, *incredibile dictu*, I never met anybody who refused to help me in the best way he or she could. And this, over two continents and through at least eight different nations. Certainly I have contracted, with them all, a debt that I will never be able to pay in full. If only for this, I would dare to say that I have been a man smiled upon by Fortune. And here, indeed, I take the liberty of disturbing Clio to give her my most humble thanks.

R.L.

Acknowledgments

I wish to thank Mr. Howell Erwin, of Athens, Georgia, who kindly—in a truly Southern *grand seigneur* style—allowed me to freely use the Cobb Collection and its invaluable papers, now housed in the University of Georgia Library. The same should be said of the personnel and staffs of the following archives: University of Georgia, Athens, Georgia; Clemson University Library, Clemson, South Carolina; South Caroliniana Collection, Columbia, South Carolina; South Carolina Historical Society Library, Charleston, South Carolina; Charleston Library Society, Charleston, South Carolina; Southern Historical Collection, North Carolina University Library, Chapel Hill, North Carolina; North Carolina State Department of Archives and History, Raleigh, North Carolina; Virginia Historical Society Library, Richmond, Virginia; Confederate Memorial Literary Society Library, Richmond, Virginia; Virginia State Archives, Richmond, Virginia; William and Mary College Library, Williamsburg, Virginia; Library of Congress, Washington, D.C.; National Archives, Washington, D.C.; Archivo General de Indias, Sevilla, Spain; Archives de la Marine, Paris, France; as well as many other archives and repositories.

Contents

The Rise and Fall
of the Plantation South

1

The Italian Renaissance and the New World

The cultural history of the Old South has a remote source; strange as it may seem, its deepest roots are found in Italy. It may appear paradoxical (and, in a way, it is), but no genuine understanding of southern civilization can be achieved without unraveling the deep and not easily detected ties between it and the Italian classicism of the Renaissance (and, through the Renaissance, to the classical cultures of both Rome and Greece).

When the Europeans moved to "discover" and conquer the New World, they were totally under the spell of what Henri Hauser and Augustin Rénaudet adroitly called *la maîtrise italienne*. Europe, indeed, had "found" America well before Columbus, but it had not yet "discovered" America. When the Norsemen set foot on the far shore of "Vinland," the civilization of the Middle Ages was at high noon in Europe. Both the Holy Roman Empire and the Universal Church of Roman Catholicism held sway over the Continent; the European economy was still mainly agricultural; feudalism was in its heyday, with its ideals of chivalry, status, ease of living, and large land tenures. That world was perfect-in-itself; Aristotle and Ptolemy had clearly stated its philosophical and geographical features:

15

the "Hemisphere of Earth" on one side, with its center the Holy See (and the Holy Empire, brightened by the Church's light, as the Moon by the Sun); the "Hemisphere of Water" on the concealed side, past the Herculean columns, toward the sunset. Two centuries after the Norsemen's arrival in "Vinland," Dante still considered it blasphemous to try to go "to the back of sunlight, where no man lives"; and in *The Inferno*, Ulysses, who tried, nevertheless, was duly sent to break his neck against God's wrath, symbolized by the tall and rocky Purgatory mountain.

For this venture, Dante did not casually choose a man from the old classical world, a Greek. Why not send a Venetian or a Genoese sailor, whom his *Inferno* surely does not lack? Because the idea of "another world," "yonder," was not Christian but classical. On the other side of the Herculean columns, wrote Plato, there is an island "greater than Libya and Asia put together. . . . Because all this sea, which lies on our side [of the columns] looks like a narrow harbor; but the other one should be considered a true sea, and the land beyond, a continent. . . ." And Lucius Annaeus Seneca wrote: "A time will come . . . when Ocean shall lay open, to show an immense land. . . ." [1]

Dante, indeed, knew his classics well. The legend that the Middle Ages had no knowledge of classical writers, whose discovery is supposed to have been made by the Renaissance, has long since been dismissed as utterly false. However, this statement, like the criticism of the idea that before Columbus the New World was totally unknown, requires qualification. Dante did know several classical writers, among them Vergil, Ovid, Horace, Cicero. However, the true difference between the Middle Ages and the Renaissance was that during the former men did not appreciate classical culture according to its own scale of values; wherever classical writers did not suit the teachings of the Church, they were read in an allegorical way, so as to force them to agree with the Scriptures. So it was that Rome and its Ecumenical Empire were supposed to have been created by God's will to pave the way for the Ecumenical Church; that Vergil was interpreted as a kind of a magician or a prophet who predicted the coming of Jesus Christ; and that Ovid's rather lewd poems were read allegorically with quite another meaning.

The Renaissance brought a clear awareness that neither Greek nor Roman civilizations had been set up by the Almighty to open the way to Catholicism; that they, indeed, had nothing to do with Catholic ethics but were instead totally pagan and extraneous (if not diametrically opposite) to Christian faith and *Weltanschauung*. Consequently, pure classicism had a momentous rebirth in Italy between the end of the fourteenth century and the middle of the fifteenth. With the return of classicism came the concepts that man, not God, was the center of the world (even the Humanists who were—or professed to be—good Catholics advocated this view); that laymen, not friars or priests, were to become the social *beau idéal*; that *studia humanitatis*—and not *studia divinitatis*—had to be the main aim of an accomplished gentleman.

Along with this change came a tremendous *essor* of the bourgeoisie (in part generated by it, in part as a cause of its own). The bourgeois class had had its origins in the northern Italian city-states immediately after the turn of the first millennium. In opposition to the agricultural ideals of the feudal world, burgeois ideals derived from those of living in cities. In the cities the people organized new, embryonic states, free communes; there they developed the main bourgeois activities: industrial production, trade, banking, shipping. From Italy, Italian bankers (such as the Medicis at Lyon), Italian intellectuals, philosophers, sailors, and geographers spread all over Europe, which, from Lisbon to the river Elbe, from Sicily to England, was caught up in the whirlwind of the Italian "cultural revolution."

Everywhere feudal society was in its twilight. Everywhere the new bourgeois class was trying to rise to power. Outside Italy, the absolute monarchies were ready to accept the help of the bourgeoisie, at least enough to curb the domination of feudal lords. However, the bourgeois class was not yet mature enough; its day was still to come. Nowhere was the bourgeoisie able to organize itself on a nationwide basis. In Italy, where no centralized government existed, the bourgeoisie was too strong to accept any leadership by a king, but not strong enough to unify the whole peninsula. Italy was the true mind of the cultural revolution—albeit a mind with no body. Italian intellectuals quickly acquired universal connotations and gave cultural leadership to the European revolution as a whole. Outside Italy the bourgeois class was not strong enough—either economically or culturally—to seize political leadership; consequently, it had to compromise with old medieval institutions, the absolute monarchies, the gentry, even the Church. Instead of complete leadership, the bourgeois class achieved at least a major control of economic and financial power: political, military, and charismatic power remained in the hands of the kings, the gentry, and the Church (even though these institutions had gone through deep transformations in comparison to the Middle Ages, sometimes at the cost of a religious schism as in England or of a reform as in Germany).

Be that as it may, it was not the merchant but the knight who best embodied the living ideal of the *integralis homo* of the Renaissance. Such Renaissance knights, not so powerful as the old feudal warlords had been, devoted servants to their kings, not disdainful of good money, cultivated and daring, were ready for a new expansionistic cycle, which had to be their own, as the Crusades had been for feudal lords. In both cases, the bourgeois class was to contribute both the economic impulse and the money.

So the stage was set for the major drama of "discovery." Spearheaded by Italian sailors,[2] financed by Italian bankers (Columbus's voyage was made thanks to the money given by a syndicate of three major Genoese banks), the Europeans were now ready to accept, even scientifically, the idea of a "New World" beyond the ocean, full of riches, of wonders, waiting to be discovered, conquered, subdued, Christianized, and, last but not least, even exploited.

It was the culture of the Italian Renaissance that first landed on the New World's fateful shores. And not only because of Columbus (Cristoforo Colombo, as his name is spelled in Italy) or of Giovanni da Verrazzano (consistently misspelled Ver-

18

razano) or of either Caboto or Vespucci. There was certainly a deep meaning in the simple fact that a son of Italy was to discover the New World, but this is not the point. The point is that the men who later came to the New World were either Renaissance knights (some, like Cortés, were; others like Pizarro, were not) or men who had imbibed, directly or indirectly, the ideal spirit of the true "Renaissance Knight" as described in 1528 by Baldassare Castiglione in his book *The Courtier* [3] and were living, literally, as in a dream, in an era of an inspired classical revival.

As we shall see later, England, more than any other country except Italy, had absorbed in full the classical ideals of the Italian Renaissance; however, on the shores of the New World, the Britons were to be latecomers. Spaniards and Frenchmen arrived earlier. Both Spanish and French societies were, if anything, aristocratic and hierarchic. Their *caballeros* and *gentilshommes* represented the very embodiment of the Renaissance "individual man." Their culture was classical from top to bottom. When another Italian, Pietro Martire d'Anghiera, set out to narrate the epics of discovery and conquest, it was not by chance that the exploits of the explorers seemed to him like revivals of Vergil's *Aeneid*, similar to expeditions by "new Greeks" from European shores toward the "new Italy" beyond the ocean. Here are, for instance, Columbus and his men landing in the New World, as depicted by Pietro Martire: "They found there several kings, as we read of the fabulous Aenes, who found Latium divided between Latinus, Mezentius, Turnus and Tarchon, separated by borders over small territories. . . ." [4]

Actually, Columbus had indicated the way. In his letter to the sovereigns of Castile, he began by invoking the cliché of the New World as a second Garden of Eden; Verrazzano, in his turn, was imbued by Arcadian legends and myths; [5] both he and Columbus, in describing the New World, freely mixed landscapes similar to those of Dante's earthly Paradise with others recalling the fabulous gardens of the Hesperides. [6]

In both Spain and France the gentry still had the decisive word as far as political affairs were concerned, and the bourgeois and mercantile classes were still playing a hidden role. Surely, both the Fuggers of Augsburg and the Medicis of Lyon thought more of the fur trade and gold imports than of any other concern. On the other hand, the political élite of the conquerors soon set forth to organize in the New World a hierarchic society founded on land *seigneurie*, as in Europe. The new overseas empires had to be mainly agricultural, based on land owned by "cavaliers" and governed with political astuteness, not by commercial greed. Trade, certainly, was granted a very important part in the life of the new colonies; indeed, it was trade that was given the rather difficult task of sating the seemingly inexhaustible thirst for gold of the mother countries, but its place, nevertheless, had to be subordinated.

This agrarian, seigneurial civilization, haunted by classical ghosts, quickly engulfed what was to become the Old South. When, after a merciless struggle to oust French intruders, Pedro Menéndez de Avilés built up the maritime strategic system of Spain to dominate the Atlantic, the future South had a prominent part in it. From that moment on, the presence of Spanish *caballeros* and friars in Florida, Georgia, and even South Carolina was to be felt for years to come. They modified both fauna and flora; they introduced tobacco, rice, peaches, sea-island cotton; they immediately organized the land in seigneurial and missionary tenures, thus creating a true hothouse for the development of a future agrarian, seigneurial society.[7]

It was this kind of America that glittered before the eyes of eager sailors and knights from England, who, by the middle of the sixteenth century, were dreaming of emulating both Columbus and Cortés. As previously observed, England was fully saturated with Italian Renaissance culture. English pupils, beginning in grammar school, were well versed in Latin through close study of Ovid, Terence, Cicero, Sallust, and Vergil. The English language was even being latinized, as was to be seen in writers from Shakespeare to Milton. In such ways, a *Weltanschauung* far different from the medieval concept was being instilled into English minds. As Wallace Notestein wrote, later it was to be "a complaint of the Puritans . . . that the boys were taught a pagan morality." [8] Italian humanists, such as John Florio, were held in high esteem in England: "the intellectual world in which the reading and thinking Englishman lived was not far behind that of Italy and was almost abreast of that in Germany and France." [9] Those who could not read Latin had at their disposal many excellent translations from classical authors; Stoic philosophy was receiving a wide audience; even country preachers were accustomed to quoting from Cicero's *De Officiis*. Those working for a bachelor of arts degree had to study the works of Quintilian and Aristotle in addition to rhetoric and logic, the fundamental disciplines.

This England—leaning to classicism, versed in Latin and Greek authors to the point of being not far behind Italy, latinizing its own language, host to many an Italian humanist—was indeed ready to accept and eagerly digest the classical image of the New World as pictured by Columbus, Verrazzano, and Pietro Martire. This, not so much because the first English voyage to the New World had been made by an Italian, Giovanni Caboto; not even because in 1516 Sir Thomas More had given to the press his *Libellus de optimo reipublicae statu deque Nova Insula Utopia;* but mainly thanks to a second-rate writer, but first-rate humanist, Richard Eden, geographer, cosmographer, humanist, and Latinist. In 1555 Eden published *The Decades of the Newe Worlde, or West India, written in the Latine tounge by Peter Martyr of Angleria,* a translation of the first three *Decades* by Pietro Martire, plus several other texts, which gave the English people the classical Italian image of America.[10] In 1577 Eden's successor, Richard Willes, published a condensed version of the remaining *Decades,* as *The History of Trauayle in the West and East Indies and other countreys. . . .*[11] Consequently, pre-Elizabethan English society, seigneurial if any was, early absorbed the classical interpretation of the New World set out by the Italian Renaissance; an interpretation fitting perfectly with aristocratic ideals.

In 1556, one year after the publication of Eden's work, a distinguished Venetian humanist, Giambattista Ramusio, published the third volume of a remarkable work: the first universal collection of documents relating to travels and discoveries, *Delle Navigazioni e Viaggi.* This volume, actually the third but printed as the second, was dedicated to *Le Nauigationi nel Mondo Nuovo, à gli Antichi incognito*.[12] Ramusio's "literary history" was really the epic of discovery. He was a true representative of the aristocratic Renaissance civilization. A Latinist, humanist, politician, geographer, and historian, he corresponded with Baldassare Castiglione, the author who had created the true model of the modern knight. In a short while, Ramusio's book became a true bible (and more than a Bible) to English geographers and sailors, mainly through the work of a man whose destiny would soon be that of giving an ideological framework to the Elizabethan image of America: Richard Hakluyt the younger.

As F. M. Rogers observed, Hakluyt had a remarkable "ability to read both printed and manuscript works in Greek, Latin, Italian, Spanish, 'Portugall' and French." [13] Hakluyt had eagerly read the narrative by Verrazzano, as published by Ramusio: to him—as to other learned Englishmen who were by now well acquainted with Martire—Verrazzano gave new ideas, new images of the New World in a more classical and Arcadian vein, very suitable to a civilization still founded upon the prevalence of landed gentlemen. Under Hakluyt's stimulus, the remaining *Decades* by Martire (from fourth to eightieth), untouched by Eden, were translated by Michael Lok.[14]

Nourished by such literature, inspired by a mentor such as Hakluyt, English discoverers moved toward the "Newe Worlde" as to a classical dreamland. In 1578 George Best, who twice commanded a ship during Frobisher's expeditions in search of a Northwest Passage, published his relation of these voyages.[15] The style was the so-called Latinate English; the tone, definitely epic. The classicism of the Italian Renaissance was beginning to shape the Elizabethan Empire in the New World. About sixty years after the publication of Sir Thomas More's *Utopia*, a full array of real Itlodeuses was leading the English wave toward America. In 1582, following the example of his beloved, worshiped Ramusio, Hakluyt gave to the press his first, and shorter, collection, the *Divers Voyages*. There is a concealed link between Plato, Seneca, More, Ramusio, and Hakluyt the younger.

Now leapt on stage those two whose destiny was to shape forever a classical America in the South: Sir Humphrey Gilbert and Sir Walter Ralegh.* Neither of them ever colonized the South. Gilbert's expedition to America ended in disaster and Ralegh never set foot on Virginia's shores, but none was more instrumental in shaping the ideology of the future southern master class.

The action of Gilbert was indirect. Almost fifteen years older than Ralegh (a kinsman of his), Gilbert was a true scion of the Tudor gentry. Well learned in Latin and Italian (he had studied at Oxford and Eton), ambitious, energetic, and restless, he early conceived plans for establishing a colony in North America. His mentor was, obviously, Richard Hakluyt the younger; indeed, Hakluyt had found "his" man in Gilbert. Very soon Gilbert brought Ralegh into his venture. It was he who persuaded Ralegh to follow his destiny. Unfortunately, Gilbert's enterprise ended in ghastly failure. His ship was swallowed by the ocean and he died like one of his beloved classical heroes whom his humanistic culture had taught him to worship: firm on the quarterdeck of his small vessel, reading in Sir Thomas More's *Utopia* the observation that, for a sailor, the distance both to earth and to heaven is the same.

So the letters-patent given by the Queen to Gilbert were inherited by Ralegh. In this way he entered upon his momentous and tragic career which, at a superficial glance, may seem a total failure. As for his Virginian empire, he never set foot in it, and the colony did not succeed; his Guiana enterprise was a dismal failure. Ruined and discredited, he ended his life on the scaffold. Nevertheless, nobody did so much to build a lasting southern civilization, nobody put on it a more permanent stamp.

* It is to be observed that the usual spelling "Raleigh" is most probably wrong, Sir Walter signing more frequently "Ralegh" (in other cases, even "Rawley," but never Raleigh). See "The Spelling of R.'s Name" in E. Thompson, *Sir Walter Ralegh, the Last of the Elizabethans*, London, 1935.

2

Ralegh,
the Renaissance Hero

No Elizabethan was more Italian than Sir Walter Ralegh. First, there was his cultural formation. Not only was he fluent in both Latin and Italian, he was also a true scholar of Italian Renaissance culture. His wide knowledge of Machiavelli is well documented. Unfortunately, the link between Machiavelli and Ralegh was originally based on false evidence. Such distinguished authors as Mario Praz, Vincent Luciani, E. A. Strathmann, and F. Rabb relied mainly on such works as *The Cabinet-Council* and *The Maxims of State*, which more recent scholarship has declared spurious, to establish the relationship. Recently Pierre Lefranc has more soundly explored the extremely important question of Machiavelli's decisive influence over Ralegh.[1]

But Ralegh was not influenced solely by Machiavelli. Other major Italian writers, the great historian Francesco Guicciardini and the philosopher Giordano Bruno, for example, had a remarkable influence on him.[2] Apart from the effect of Italian writers on him, it was more remarkable still how Ralegh managed to embody the Renaissance ideal of the *integralis homo*. To begin with, his life and character were both epitomes of Baldassare Castiglione's theme in his book *The Courtier*.

The noble ideal of serving a prince with dignity, honor, and distinction, adding brightness to the prince's court and being brightened by it, was Ralegh's own. This choice exposed him to a risky, wonderful, exceptional life in a truly heroic, almost superhuman atmosphere; and the fiery daily clash between his courageous *natur* (or his *virtu*) and *fortuna* (in the Latin meaning of the blind goddess of chance) made of him one of the more perfect realizations of Machiavellian heroes. He felt the struggle dramatically and described it as ending by,

> Levinge each withered boddy to be torne
> By fortune, and by tymes tempestius,
> Which by her vertu, once faire frute have borne . . .[3]

As the scholarly editor of Ralegh's verses wrote, "There is and always has been something legendary, something fantastic and not quite credible about him. Even to his contemporaries he seemed a man of more than normal stature: so monstrously proud, so dangerously subtle, and in the end so horribly wronged. . . . He might have walked out of an Elizabethan play, a figment of the renaissance imagination, compact of inordinate vice and virtues and destined to strange ends." [4]

Ralegh longed for glory, striving for wealth not out of sheer greed but for the noble status that wealth would bring him; he would spend it, not hoard it. He brooded over great, almost Promethean projects; but at the same time he was fighting to rise among Elizabethan courtiers, planning heroic enterprises, studying and meditating over the masterpieces of history, philosophy, poetry, Latin, writing verses, and all this with an ease that totally justifies the desperate cry uttered by a spectator during the tragic night when he was executed: "Where should we find another such head to cut off?" [5]

Far from England, in Italy, where Renaissance civilization was flourishing, such men as Leon Battista Alberti, Baldassare Castiglione, Pietro Bembo, and Niccolò Machiavelli were dreaming of such an aristocratic knight: an ideal only imperfectly realized in the culturally great, but politically weak, peninsula. Only far afield, over the mighty and immense ocean, in the boundless "Newe Worlde," where any phenomenon seemed to be on a gigantic scale, was such an ideal to become a reality. Indeed, even the Italians who had best embodied it had been Cristoforo Colombo, Giovanni da Verrazzano, Amerigo Vespucci, and Giovanni Caboto, true knights-errant of new epic poems, sons of a civilization that, if more and more linked with the growing bourgeoisie, was nevertheless still landholding, aristocratic, and heroic in its true aspirations. Such a knight-errant was Ralegh, wishing

To seeke new worlds, for golde, for prayse, for glory . . .[6]

Ralegh, Gilbert, and their mentor, Hakluyt, were daydreaming over the history of Greek and Roman colonizations as recorded by Machiavelli,[7] planning to create something similar on the wide shores of the semifantastic New World. Such Roman inspiration for Hakluyt's schemes for colonizing America was to be clearly stated by another Italian philosopher, Giambattista Vico, a hundred years later: ". . . colonies, were to be, first, groups of laborers and farmers tilling distant lands in order to secure supplies to military gentry; then, gentlemen, having fields cultivated for their own benefit. . . ."[8] This clearly stated the two phases of the seigneurial colonization envisaged by Hakluyt.[9]

When Gilbert died, Ralegh was left to attempt on his own the realization of these plans. Acting alone did not intimidate him; indeed, he had been born to fight alone. Great individuals of the Renaissance, as Jacob Burckhardt wrote, were men ". . . wonderfully energetic and versatile, able to assimilate at a single stroke any cultural aspect of their age"; such was the *homo universalis*, who was "peculiarly Italian."[10] Such was Ralegh, in the daily heroic struggle of his "virtue" against the tempestuous winds of "fortune." He was to be frequently prostrated, but his work was to survive—and change the world's and mankind's future.

Machiavelli had set the stage for the immense political drama of the Renaissance. Along with other Machiavellian *dramatis personae*, Ralegh was true to his glorious and tragic fate:

26

And (my) only joye that Fortune conquers Kinges;
Fortune, that rules the Earth and earthly thinges,
Hathe ta'en my love, in spighte of vertues mighte:
So blinde a goddess did never vertue righte.[11]

Nevertheless, he—like all great players—had a kind of reliance on fortune:

Knowinge she cann renew, and cann create
Green from the grovnde, and floures, yeven out of stone,
By vertu lastinge over tyme and date . . .[12]

So he went onward, seeing clearly the final tragedy that was to overthrow him. After several failures, no more "golde," "prayse," or "glory" were to be seen beyond the dark horizon, and Ralegh knew this:

My hopes cleane out of sight, with forced wind
To kyngdomes strange, to lands far off addrest . . .[13]

Indeed, fate was against him. Ralegh never set foot on his "roman" colony, on his Virginia. However, he cast over that hallowed land such an immense shadow that Virginia (and the whole South) is still living, consciously or not, under its spell. From the exquisite, aristocratic culture of the Italian Renaissance he drew and embodied in an almost perfect way the ideal of the noble courtier-cavalier.

During his whole life he had been true to his mighty aim; he had been the classic, "Italian" hero of England and America, the man who, by his titanic, if erratic, will, had transplanted to the far shores of the "Newe Worlde" the kind of classical, agrarian colony that Machiavelli and Hakluyt had been dreaming of. To his colony he gave forever, as an ideal, as an object of self-identification, as an ideology, the myth of the "Sir Knight," which was to shape the mind and inform the *Weltanschauung* of the South.

The Ideological Basis
for Sectional Cultures

The so-called Pilgrim Fathers did not land in Virginia—and this was not by chance. To speculate on what might have happened had they landed at Jamestown is purely a waste of time. History went as it went, and not as it might have gone. At any rate, the "Pilgrims" settled in Massachusetts. Objectively, they were a very mixed array; they did not even know they were the "Pilgrim Fathers." The name was given to them by nineteenth-century historians. However, the real, the transcendental importance of Plymouth's settlement was that it opened the way for the great Puritan wave that followed several years later.

Let us not be concerned, for the time being, with the economic base of the puritan oligarchy. It has been said and re-said that the Puritans were a bourgeois vanguard, that their social base was bourgeois-capitalist, and this is undoubtedly true. But this truth requires some qualification. As it has been correctly observed, "without a careful analysis of the legal, moral, religious, and institutional inheritance and its survivals in colonial life" it is impossible to understand the peculiar story of any social formation. "The economic and ecologic processes enable us to account for the room given that inheritance to breathe." [1]

What needs to be stressed here is the singular philosophy and *Weltanschauung* that the Puritans brought with them.

Puritanism was historically akin to Calvinism; and Calvinism had its deepest foundations in the doctrines of St. Augustine, as set out in such works as *The City of God*. During his youth, St. Augustine had been a faithful adherent of Manicheism. Later, under the influence of Greek philosophy and Roman Catholicism, he became a Christian; however, the Manichean division of mankind into "sons of light" and "sons of darkness" was to reemerge dramatically in his thought when, in his mature age, he was fighting his great ideological battle against Pelagius, Bishop of the Gaules. Pelagius's doctrine, considering human nature to be healthy and free from the consequences of original sin, postulated that man's will was totally free and able to bring mankind to eternal salvation by itself. This conclusion was not surprising, as Pelagius was a follower of Greek philosophy, mainly Stoicism. St. Augustine believed such ideas to be wrong, because, for one thing, by giving an excessive power and autonomy to human reason, Pelagius would have ended by considering useless both the Church and the coming of Christ as instruments of human redemption. Pushed by an urge to give what seemed to him the deepest meaning to the sacrifice of Christ, St. Augustine moved backward, "burning" more and more what he had worshiped, and turned toward a doctrine of human predestination that was all but loathsome to the classical spirit.

The classical cultures of Greece and Rome had considered man to be the center of the universe and had underlined his total intellectual freedom (with some exception, however, in early Stoicism), founding such freedom on the rational nature of man. To St. Augustine, men seemed more and more subservient to sin and doomed to damnation except for an élite group who were granted the grace of God through a totally arbitrary choice by the Almighty. Classical culture, which St. Augustine had once relied on to build up his doctrine of intellectual freedom, became, in his mind, the paraphernalia of the "City of the Devil." "The philosopher," A. Weber wrote of him, "had bowed respectfully to Classic Virtues; the theologian could no more see in them any other thing than concealed sins, *splendida vitia*." [2]

The Catholic Church had early been aware of the potential dangers that were inherent in St. Augustine's doctrine. The major Catholic philosopher and theologian of the later Middle Ages, St. Thomas Aquinas, spent so much of his dialectic ability in clarifying and explaining what St. Augustine had "really meant" that the phrase *Augustinus eget Thoma interprete* became familiar. Afraid of seeing a doctrine of predestination creep into Catholicism through St. Augustine's ideas, St. Thomas maintained that, certainly, Pelagius was wrong. No man may achieve redemption without grace, but grace is not distributed on an arbitrary basis, for God himself (being pure and supreme reason) cannot do anything irrational or illogical. That this simply would shift determinism from human to divine reason can be sustained. However, St. Thomas's doctrine succeeded in preventing the Catholic Church from accepting a doctrine of predestination, which would have broken any link with classical tradition and culture.

The Reformation was to reject St. Thomas's philosophy, and return to St. Augustine's, as more congenial. In his old age, St. Augustine had moved dangerously close to the Manicheism of his youth, although without relapsing into it. In the later Middle Ages, a protean heresy had appeared throughout Europe: Catharism. The ubiquitous Catharist groups preached predestination and a sharp division of mankind into "saints" and "sinners." The "saints," obviously, were the Catharists themselves. The Catholic Church quickly identified Catharists as Manicheists, but only recently has it been possible to find in the records of the Middle Ages a clear, explicit allusion to Mani by Catharists.[3]

The contributions of Catharism are almost impossible to measure, but it was certainly an important influence on the characters of such heretical sects of the Middle Ages as Albigensianism, Vaudois, Lollardy, and others. The followers of such groups usually entered Calvinist churches, to which they brought a strong Catharistic tendency. This encouraged in

Calvinism a fully Manichean interpretation of St. Augustine's thought, through which the old doctrine of the division of mankind into "sons of light" and "sons of darkness" had a revival at the very brink of the Modern Era. This was a doctrine that repudiated all that was classical and Roman (and also, as a matter of fact, the classicism of the Renaissance).

So it was that Calvinism remained watertight to the influence of Renaissance classicism. Certainly, the author of the *Institutio Religionis Christianae* paid lip service to classicism: he was, after all, a son of his age. But he strongly denied any value whatsoever to "pagan" ethics. Hulric Zwingli, who did not want to give up his humanist learning, tried to frame a doctrine of "spiritual predestination to Salvation" so that the major poets and philosophers of Greece and Rome might be included, together with Hebrews and Christians, among the "saints" or, at least, the likely-to-be-sanctified; but Calvin abruptly dismissed such "fanciful ideas." Indeed, he rejected more strongly than St. Augustine any reliance on classical culture, and to find the very foundations of his new *Civitas Dei*, he turned from the New Testament to the Ancient One. In doing so, he put completely aside ten centuries of classical civilization.

This kind of suspicion and scorn of classicism permeated English Puritanism from its very beginnings, inasmuch as the hated Established High Church was as prone as Roman Catholicism to Roman tradition and as ready to swallow the bait of classical culture. The basic ideological differences between Virginia and New England reflected this pattern. The former had been generated as the legitimate daughter of English Renaissance culture; the latter was anti-classic: to it, indeed, classicism and *studia humanitatis* always were—and had to be —*splendida vitia* to be anathematized.

So it was that both classical culture and ethics, which had been present at the very birth of Virginia, did not cross the ocean on Pilgrim and Puritan ships. "True sons of the Renaissance, the early Virginians read the classics for pleasure and to understand the past and present," [4] whereas their New England counterparts were only reading and printing Bibles. After all, might two civilizations have so distant and different fathers as Sir Walter Ralegh—and John Calvin?

The Renaissance had to wait for two centuries more before entering New England; the great literary wave that traveled all over that country during the first half of the nineteenth century was appropriately named a "renaissance." It was truly a late-coming stepdaughter of the great era. But, strange to say, when the Renaissance at last reached New England, it did so in peculiar garb, similar to old puritanical intolerance but disguised as a classical robe.

When the Puritans came to America in the seventeenth century, the old struggle between "saints" and "demons" was simply transported across the Atlantic. However, for the time being, the "saints" had their hands full. Their thirst for "demons" to fight against was more than satisfied by French "papists" and "devilish" Indians, as well as their own witches. Seen from the distance of time it is clear that the ideology upon which New England was built was, at any rate, the absolute reverse of the ideology of Virginia. This may seem (and, certainly, in part is) an oversimplification; however, it gives, I suppose, a fair idea of the opposite ideologies that underlay the sectional conflict of America.

Certainly, the development of New England's colonies was distinctly different from the southern experience. New England was fast becoming a land of thrifty merchants, shipmasters, and bankers, inspired by the idea of a divine mission, accustomed to humbling themselves before an overpowering God, but, in the meantime, often terribly arrogant, as is usual with righteous men, whose arrogance goes hand in hand with humility.

In the South, Renaissance "gentlemen" believed in a strong individuality and defied adverse fortune by personal virtue. Habitual seigneurs of large land-holdings, without any strong religious discipline, they were fond of good reading, leisure, hunting, and horsemanship. With almost no banking, scarce shipping, and no capitalist faith in predestination, there was little trade outside the selling of their tobacco crops. Certainly, such "gentlemen" had been, at the beginning, mainly men of the lower class: the idea of a Virginia populated by noblemen is a legend. However, Virginia colonists were moving in a cultural atmosphere that gave them such conditioning; those lower-class men who first came to the Virginia shore were like seeds sown over a land deeply enriched by classical Renaissance culture. Viriginia was the hothouse where such a seigneurial caste was to grow.

While the society in New England was insulated, that of the South was not. The South—as well as other American colonies founded by Spain, Portugal, and France—was socially a scion of the seigneurial class of Europe. Ideologically it was a scion of the Italian Renaissance; and, as England was under the spell of such culture more than Spain or Portugal, this was truer of English southern colonies than of Latin-American colonies (not forgetting, however, the wide dissemination of Erasmian doctrines throughout New Spain).

The peculiar religious incredulity of Renaissance Italy was certainly not widely seen in the American colonies; latitudinarianism, however, prevailed more often than not. As a matter of fact, the only examples of states founded on religious intolerance were in New England (with the partial exception of Rhode Island); the only colonies where Italian classicism was consciously refused.[5]

Certainly, New England's "priests" and "saints" were frequently good Latinists, but this must not mislead us. In that era, anybody with any pretension to even a simple cultural background read Latin. Howard Mumford Jones seems right when he writes (quoting Shakespeare's *The Tempest*): "It is virtually impossible to imagine a New England Puritan exclaiming:

O, wonder!
How many goodly creatures are there here!
How beauteous mankind is! O brave new world,
That has such people in it!

The New England mind simply did not work that way. Its New World was for the saints, not for lovers, and it failed to find most of mankind beauteous." [6]

So it was also, as far as the fine arts were concerned. The violent puritan rejection of images all but denied the enjoyment of the splendid semi-pagan paintings of the Catholic world, which were, instead, always appreciated in Virginia and the South. Very soon, the textbooks on which New England and Virginia based the intellectual education of their sons came to a sharp division. If the Bible was read in both parts of burgeoning British North America, one should never forget that the Book was usually looked at by Puritans through the lens of Calvin's *Institutio* (and St. Augustine's *De Civitate Dei*), while the fast-developing new "Virginia gentry" looked at the Bible from the standpoint of Baldassare Castiglione's *Il Cortegiano* and Machiavelli's *Il Principe*. The ideals of Canadian *gentils-hommes*, of Virginia gentlemen, of New Spain's *conquistadores* were shaped by Machiavelli for the heroic code and by Castiglione for the gentlemanly perspective.

There existed a sharp difference between ideological frames of reference. Ideologies, however, are based on a social and economic structure. In New England the structure was formed by the rising bourgeoisie. There is certainly a deep meaning in the puritan rejection of absolutistic, seigneurial England, as well as in the sense of continuity with the philosophy of the mother country that was felt by the Virginians. The old seigneurial system had its continuance in the New World through the South, New France, New Spain, and Brazil, while New England had been founded on the radical rejection of such a system.

4

New France, Cornerstone of the Seigneurial Society

Although in many parts of Latin America the seigneurial regime had begun to grow in the first years of the sixteenth century (and, in the Spanish Caribbean, it was discernible already at the end of the fifteenth), seigneurial America reached its peak only in the seventeenth and eighteenth centuries. However different the external conditions, both Americas, from French Canada down to Spanish South America, showed striking structural similarities. The exceptions were New England and the so-called Middle Colonies (New York, New Jersey, Pennsylvania), which were bourgeois and capitalist. Everywhere the foundation of society was agriculture, mainly based on large-scale land property; everywhere a distinctive single-crop or single-staple economy prevailed (furs in French Canada; tobacco, rice, and indigo in the southern English colonies; sugar in the Caribbean and in Brazil). Everywhere (with the exception of French Canada, where later we will see the exception that confirms the rule) slavery was the dominant labor system; everywhere the social body was ruled by a particular class, agricultural, paternalistic, more similar in its social connotations to European nobility than to the bourgeoisie, with whom, indeed, it had nothing in common.

Recently two distinguished authors, Robert W. Fogel and Stanley Engerman, in their much-discussed book *Time on the Cross*, have tried to describe what they call "the economics of slavery" by means of an econometric analysis. They reach the somewhat surprising conclusion that the slaveholding class was simply capitalistic. I have no intention here of entering the polemic (or squabble) over that work. It has indeed been completely and carefully criticized by many writers, who have clearly shown the inconsistency of developing a "new" historiography by making absolute what amounts simply to a new (and not so new) heuristic tool. They have questioned the incongruency of jumping from doubtful and clearly partial findings to what are, in some cases, hasty and arbitrary conclusions that are in no way supported by the data; and the feebleness of these very data cannot sustain close mathematical scrutiny.[1] However, two points need to be stressed here.

First of all, "slavery" is, in itself, an abstraction. There is no such thing as "slavery"—there are only *slave societies*, which means that slavery cannot be isolated from the whole context of the society and class relations to which it belongs. Such societies must be considered throughout the space and time dimensions. In other words, is there a similarity between slave societies (if any existed) in the Ancient and in the New World? Is there any similarity between contemporaneous slave societies in Africa and the Americas? Without trying to analyze this question, a sound study of any given slave society is utterly impossible. More than one hundred years ago, Hegel cogently demonstrated the absurdity of pretending to isolate the individual personality from the social one and social dimensions from their historic background.

The second observation is that the authors of *Time on the Cross*, who are speaking only of slavery in the southern United States (and should have said so), seem guilty of a second arbitrary reduction when they speak of the South. They intend, really, to confront only a fragment of its history, including a few score years immediately prior to the Civil War, the so-called cotton era of the South. This is, as we shall see, the most important point, as here the authors try to demonstrate the assumed capitalist character of southern planters. Let us put aside the clumsy and awkward argument that southerners were "capitalists" because they "made money." If any society able to produce a surplus should be considered "capitalistic," capitalism would begin in the Stone Age and become truly the Hegelian "night where any cow looks dark." But, as history should contrive to clarify, and not to obscure, this argument should be set aside as useless and harmful.[2]

Slavery was introduced into the Americas by capitalism. Mercantile capitalism was the powerful engine that propelled Europe toward America; capitalistic interests backed the enterprises of Columbus (which, as noted earlier, had been financed by three major Genoese banks); capitalism opened the European markets to Canadian furs, Brazilian and Caribbean sugar, and Virginia's tobacco. Capitalism was the prime engine that built up a major network of colonies, naval bases, trading interests. But no capitalist class was yet in power in Europe to spearhead the expansionist movement, to build up colonial empires, to defend, administer, and govern them. The bourgeois class had to rely on the old-fashioned institutions that had been born in the feudal Middle Ages: absolute monarchies, military aristocracies, universal churches. These were the builders of the political, military, and ideological framework of American empires, those which gave them their characteristic seigneurial ruling classes (with the only exception, as already noted, the bourgeois colonies founded by English Puritans and Dutch Calvinists). Slavery quickly became the solution for exploiting such enormous territories; it even fit well with the old-fashioned agricultural minds of local seigneurs; and the slave trade soon opened to bourgeois classes prospects of tremendous profits. One has only to peruse the documents collected and edited by Elizabeth Donnan to be persuaded that the slave trade—not slavery—was what primarily interested bourgeois capitalists.[3] Soon Portuguese, English, Dutch, and French slavers inundated the Americas with black Africans, far surpassing the real needs of local planters, who even tried to stop this uninterrupted flow of blacks, but to no avail.[4]

Certainly, seigneurs needed slaves in order to have cheap,

well-disciplined workers; slavery even suited the individual frame of mind, which was paternalistic and authoritarian. Add that this was the only way to exploit large landholdings throughout the New World (agrarian capitalism based on wage laborers and a heavy investment in agricultural machines was yet to be born; it comes usually only *after* industrial capitalism, when huge development of a sophisticated technology permits major investments of capital per acre, not only in machines, but also in fertilizer, canals, drainage, and skilled labor, similar to the industrial kind).

All over the world, the capitalist classes were fighting for power. The English, American, and French revolutions would finally bring them to the helm; they would no longer need any further support from old-fashioned medieval classes, which, instead, they would sweep away by "blood and iron." The bourgeois historian Francis Parkman appropriately described the struggle between England (and New England), on one hand, and France (and New France), on the other, as the struggle of "modern society against the Middle Ages." The French-American seigneurial society was defeated, the first to succumb to the blows of the new, powerful capitalist society. Then, however, the winners found next door other old-fashioned seigneurial societies, those founded upon slavery.

Capitalism had been instrumental in introducing slavery into the Americas. There, as Eugene D. Genovese adroitly pointed out, slavery had become the base on which had been built a powerful seigneurial system. And now capitalism was finding such societies its neighbors. History plays such tricks on men!

However powerful and complex, however widespread and developed, slave societies were still helplessly dependent on capitalism. Since approximately A.D. 1000, when it had been born in northern Italian towns, capitalism had been building a worldwide network of trade interests, a general regulator of economy and prices: the world market. Through it, capitalism economically dominated the whole earth. Very few—if any—societies were able to escape the iron laws of the capitalist world market. It fast reduced any backward agricultural society to a colonial or quasi-colonial status of dependency. Such societies were superficially free to decide their own economic policies, but, as a matter of fact, they were actually compelled to submit to the demands of the capitalist world market.

In this way, any semicolonial country was forced into a single-crop status; a diversification of cultures, which is the basis of independence, because it affords the possibility of resisting pressures from outside, even blockades, was all but impossible. The mother country supplied all other products; all the land not involved in single-crop agriculture was doomed to produce no profit since the world market, which avidly absorbed the single staple, was all but closed to any other product. The defense of their interest forced planters, *fazendeiros*, *hacendados*, and *gentilshommes* to yield. And what was more important, the capitalist world market not only imposed single-crop status, it even dictated what kind of staple had to be produced. Near the end of the eighteenth century the industrial revolution in England created an immense demand for cotton. This, not the invention of the cotton gin, was the true cause that transformed the Lower South (and part of Brazil) into the "cotton kingdom." The demand from the world market was so pressing that had Eli Whitney been unable to invent the gin, somebody else would have done so: "the need creates the organ."

Consequently, before the Civil War, the South felt the effect of a clear economic trend in the world market that was setting a high premium on cotton. While it is almost impossible to speculate on how long this situation would have continued without the Civil War, it is to be emphasized here that to judge southern economics by a particular combination of circumstances, which, in all, lasted not more than thirty years (out of two hundred and fifty of the life of the Old South), seems a strange way indeed to attempt to understand the nature of a given society. The plantation system was backward; no witness ever doubted that this was the case. Its productivity was not "high" and its efficiency was, at best, doubtful. "Today, Kuwait may well have the highest per capita income in the world. Does this reflect economic development, efficient Kuwaitian labor, or world demand for oil coupled with a producer's near monopoly, as in the case of the cotton South?" [5] Speaking of another remarkable seigneurial society, New France, William J. Eccles wrote: " . . . the tendency . . . to pass judgment on a country, colony or society in purely economic terms . . . can lead to bizarre conclusions. In Canada, when wheat production fell off and food had to be imported, a sharp increase in shipping resulted. Conversely, crop failures in France caused an increase of shipping from Canada to the other colonies. Thus, had there been more frequent crop failures in the empire, the volume of shipping would have been greater, and economic activity [would have] appeared more flourishing. . . . These dubious economic statistics are a poor measure of the quality of life." [6]

In the seventeenth and eighteenth centuries no "cotton South" existed; however, the southern seigneurial society was there, fully developed and adult. Let us try to analyze it more closely, setting it against the framework of the New World's seigneurial societies of the same era. The starting point has to be the *Weltanschauung* of the seigneurial class. As Eugene D. Genovese remarked, "an ideological and psychological assessment of the southern slaveholders is essential to an understanding of southern political economy." [7]

To begin with, the seigneurial system was by no means based everywhere upon slavery. In part of Mexico, for instance, even in parts of the so-called Spanish Main, Negro slavery was more limited. Indian *peons* were good surrogates for African slaves; equally, a close study of the habits, ideology, tastes, etc., of Spanish-American *hacendados* shows them to have been very close to southern planters and Brazilian *fazendeiros*. Economically, too, the machinery of haciendas was akin to those of plantations, a subject that will be pursued later.

Any inquiry into the seigneurial classes should begin with New France. Close scrutiny reveals it to have been the true cradle and cornerstone of this type of society. In French Canada slavery was a very limited phenomenon, even if, contrary to what is usually assumed, Canada did have several thousand slaves.[8] In spite of this limited presence of slavery, Canadian society was totally seigneurial; indeed, it is from French Canada that the adjective comes. It was in

Canada that the failure to impose a wholly feudal society gave birth to the seigneurial compromise, with a character similar to those of Virginia, Brazil, the Caribbean, and most parts of the rest of Latin America.

In 1541 Francis I of France granted to the newly appointed lieutenant general of "la Nouvelle France," Jean-François de la Rocque de Roberval, the right of distributing fiefs. In a few decades, fiefs grew up all over the land. However, the "feudal" regime of New France soon showed a character of its own, a character not to be found in the Old World; consequently, the name "feudal" early appeared improper to describe it. The "seigneur" had no responsibility for armed defense, which the general government kept in its hands. He could not interfere with the traffic over the great waterway of the St. Lawrence, and his powers of justice were soon limited to petty cases. More important, he had no serfs: his *censitaires*, the so-called *habitans*, enjoyed a standard of personal freedom unknown in France, as they were not bound to the land or to their seigneur and were free to move to another place.[9] Moreover, some of the most prominent seigneurial families were not nobles, which would have been inconceivable in France under the old regime.

This freedom of the Canadian *habitans* seems very opposite to the slavery existing in the other seigneurial countries of America; still, the study and understanding of New France is the key to understanding any seigneurial society. The very magnitude and importance of slavery has obliterated, in many a historian's mind, the bare fact that everywhere slavery came "after"; plantations were born with no or little slavery, and the seigneurial classes were almost adult when slavery was introduced. In Canada this never happened, because the basic staple, furs, did not require slavery, the main task of the *habitans* being to till the land for their own and their seigneur's subsistence. Then, both seigneurs and *habitans* (these last under the name of *engagés*) dedicated themselves to fur trade with the great Indian nations living in New France. By an Express Act, Louis XIV authorized noblemen residing in Canada to engage in trade (which was strictly forbidden in their home country).[10] This contributed greatly to the involvement of the seigneurial class as business entrepreneurs, thus making its members different from members of the European feudal class, a fact that, up to today, has misled historians into mistaking them for "capitalists."

Instead, as William J. Eccles points out, ". . . the profits of fur trade were spent more on conspicuous consumption, lavish hospitality after the manner of the nobility, than they were invested in other economic endeavors. Social life in New France among the military fur-trading élite was thereby rendered urbane and agreeable, but the economy remained fragile." [11] Add to this that members of the bourgeoisie who owned seigneuries were soon ennobled.

Seigneurs very early built stately manor houses, still to be admired along the majestic St. Lawrence, where they lived a completely agrarian and patriarchal life, surrounded by their fields, mill, farmhouses of *censitaires and habitans*, frequently even huts of friendly Indians, and a chapel with a priest to celebrate mass. In his manorial house the seigneur lived as magnificently as his wealth allowed, and not infrequently more so; he kept a very liberal, permanent open house; he administered the *baisse justice*, solving small feuds between *habitans* and even between Indians, who usually called him "father," as true members of a "family" whose structure and ethics are nowhere to be found in the bourgeois and capitalist world. Power was actually in his hands; any seigneur had a military rank, down to that of captain, this last being reserved to *habitans*, whose *capitaine de milice* had the important task of maintaining the link between local seigneuries and the Real Intendant in Quebec. So the agrarian community governed itself under the superpaternalism of the king. Seigneurs and *habitans* used to mix freely with local Indians, giving birth to a large class of *métis*, or mixed-bloods, over whom the seigneur held his paternalistic sway.

Strange to say, Canada was caught in the whirlpool of the capitalist world market before the English colonies were. Exploiting the fur trade, the Canadian seigneurs were simply doing what the capitalist market wanted them to do. It was this basic contradiction that undermined the Canadian seigneurial civilization, because the fur trade, which put them on good terms with Huron and Algonquin Indians, was the main cause of the no-quarter war with the Iroquois, which, in the long run, helped overthrow the seigneurial society.

But New France was by no means limited to Canada. Down the Mississippi was that part of "la Nouvelle France" whose destiny was to be integrated into the Old South: Arkansas and the so-called Louisiana. There, too, the social structure, the ideology of the seigneurs, the way of life did not change. But sugar, not fur, was the staple, and as it was to become the future economic base of the colony, plantation slavery was soon introduced, as it was in the French Caribbean. So, Louisiana was, in a sense, the "historic link" that connected the seigneurial system of early Canada to that of the Old South. However, a close analysis of Canadian land tenure under the seigneurial regime would certainly show a rather close resemblance with the headright system of the Old South, South Carolina being clearly a case in point.[12]

Land tenure was the social base of seigneurial status throughout Canada and New France: "Despite the fact that the Canadian economy [was] basically commercial and dependent largely on the fur trade, bourgeois commercial values did not dominate society; indeed, they were scorned. . . . More than wealth, men wished to bequeath to their sons a higher social status and a name distinguished for military valor. . . ."[13]

It was, then, a society where agriculture dominated industry, as far as a scale of values was concerned. Industry was always subordinated to agricultural interests and to the will of the agrarian ruling class, who, in the main, considered the fur trade more as an occasion for moving west, hunting, fishing, and living in touch with nature than as a purely commercial venture; it was a sort of martial activity in a society where training for war was the business of every day.

Canadian seigneurial society was early defeated and almost swept away; however, a close study of it remains, as mentioned, the royal highway to understanding the intellectual aims and social ideals of the seigneurial class throughout the New World.

The "Tropical Civilization"

Even in Virginia and in the Caribbean colonies slavery was a latecomer. In the beginning, English colonists exploited their land by means of white servants;[1] in South Carolina and elsewhere, baronies of a feudal type were even organized.[2]

The first Africans had arrived in 1619, but for a long time their status was more or less mixed with that of white servants and not well defined. In Virginia the seigneurial regime was thriving before the problem of slavery made its appearance: but, being based on land cultivation and not on anything similar to the Canadian fur trade, it very soon ran into two major stumbling blocks. The first was the conflict with the Indians. Certainly, the Anglo-Saxons never learned how to deal with Indians, as the French did, even if Virginia was not addicted to the wholesale extermination of Indians as was New England. However, mutual relations need not have become so tense without the question of land ownership.[3] The second problem for the seigneurial regime was the need for a compulsory system of labor. This necessity forever prevented any possibility of good relations like those established in Canada between seigneurs and *habitans*.

Slavery, as already noted, was brought to America by capitalism. When the capitalist market began to need more and more of Virginia's tobacco and England entered the very profitable Atlantic slave trade, the English colonies of the near-tropical zone were pressed to supply more and more tobacco and to buy more and more slaves, even against their will.

Virginia, like Canada part of seigneurial America, was a member also of a more specific kind of seigneurial civilization that extended from the Chesapeake to Brazil, including the Caribbean and, in part, the Spanish Main. This civilization was adroitly called by Gilberto Freyre "tropical"; [4] and the distinguished Brazilian writer is certainly right, as its extension covers a tropical and two subtropical areas, reaching as far as the temperate zones. However, it seems more appropriate to use Jay R. Mandle's definition of "plantation civilizations" [5] so that Canada and both the hacienda civilization of the Mexican high plateaus and Argentina's large land properties, which presented very similar dimensions, can also be included. Mandle correctly underlines the fact that everywhere the end of slavery ". . . did severely shake the hegemony of the plantocracy, but its survival under formally changed circumstances of labor control, in several different countries, indicates that juridical ownership of people could be eliminated and yet the essential attributes of the plantation society be retained." [6]

Certainly what Mandle calls "plantation civilization," and what I propose to call seigneurial civilization, far exceeded the slave era both in space and time; and slave societies appear to be only the tropical species of such civilization. So we come back to Gilberto Freyre.

Slavery had entered the Americas when both English and French colonists began to establish themselves in the Caribbean. However, as in Canada and Virginia and in the Spanish colonies, the early seigneurial system in the islands belonging to both nations was based on white serfdom (the Spaniards, in their first *encomiendas*, had relied on native labor; only the physical destruction of the Indians compelled them to introduce black slavery).

The transformation of Virginia into a slave colony began when the demand for tobacco skyrocketed in the world market;

the similar transformation of the Caribbean islands was caused by another earthquake in international trade: the rise of the sugar era. The decisive way in which sugar cane became established in the New World and the clear possibility of shipping and selling sugar all over Europe made this staple a prize for traders, and the demand for sugar in the capitalist world market went literally to the stars. For whole millennia, cultivated and sophisticated European civilizations had used honey almost exclusively for sweetening; however, in the tropical climate sugar was easily produced. Together with sugar came a boom in other colonial staples, such as tea, cocoa, and coffee.[7] As raw products, they offered to mercantile capitalism the best means of exploiting the New World. Add to this that producing and exporting sugar (as Brazil clearly showed) was all but impossible without massive slave labor, and the circle—or better, the triangle—was closed. More and more sugar meant more and more slaves to be introduced by force into American markets; and if the colonists protested (as Virginians did), to hell with them! [8]

So, as previously stated, capitalism forced slavery on America. What capitalists did not suspect (and even if they had suspected it, they would not have bothered to consider the consequences) was that this would envigorate the seigneurial system of the New World, a society which, in the not too distant future, a more mature industrial capitalism would have to reckon with.

All over the zone of tropical civilization (set in train by such powerful forces) the seigneurial system prospered. Soon Barbados saw the building of stately houses where planters offered lavish and splendid hospitality to guests.[9] In Jamaica the governor, Sir Thomas Lynch, boasted a magnificent mansion of thirteen rooms, with silver services, coaches and handsome horses, a private library filled with books in English, French, Spanish, Italian, and Latin. Another beautiful and well-furnished library was that of Thomas Cradock of Port Royal, Jamaica. In comparison with Massachusetts colonists, whose libraries were filled with Bibles, lives of Cotton Mather, and other edifying books, the West Indian planters showed their humanistic taste for Latin, Italian, and French culture. Their society was strictly hierarchical; wealthy planters differentiated themselves from average and small planters and from simple freeholders, or freemen, not to speak of servants or slaves, in every way: home, clothes, food. Hierarchy was strictly observed (which is characteristic of precapitalist societies), and the ruling class was completely agrarian. By about 1685 in Barbados all offices, both civilian and military, were in the hands of planters, with an overwhelming prevalence of wealthy planters over the others. Towns were beautiful but small clusters of offices, residences of large planters and places for spending money; they were not productive centers.[10]

As in Virginia, no noblemen were to be found among the original settlers of the West Indies (although they received a not indifferent injection of pro-Stuart cavaliers during the English revolutionary era); but, as in Virginia, English country gentlemen were their ideal models, and in a few decades a complete seigneurial class arose, a class that "had built a social structure to rival the tradition-encrusted hierarchy of old England." [11]

Merchants and capitalists made a lot of money in the sugar trade, as did planters; however, they had a seigneurial, not a capitalist, philosophy. Their end was status, power, and the good life, not accumulation; so "they freely indulged in conspicuous consumption, living in a . . . showy fashion." [12]

As in other seigneurial civilizations, one of the favorite features of the Caribbean planter's life was exquisite food. The same was true of both Brazil and the Old South (which, incidentally, is still today the only section of the United States that can boast an elaborate, distinctive, rich way of cooking). *"Une civilisation, Monsieur, c'est une politesse et une cuisine,"* said Lamartine: and one might possibly understand more about the old southern civilization by the taste of gumbo, casserole, grits, and barbecue beef (and mint julep, if properly made) than by reading a large number of books. So, West Indian planters "dined richly, drank copiously, and entertained lavishly." [13]

The same was true of their French counterparts in Martinique and Santo Domingo; [14] and, as far as *hacendados* in the Spanish West Indies were concerned, one has only to see the remaining "big houses" to catch a glimpse of that incredible, dead world.

However, the West Indian world contained the fatal germs that would kill it. A seigneurial civilization is always strongly dependent on the capitalist world market. Albeit precapitalist in structure and anti-bourgeois in shape of mind, it was born *inside* a world dominated by capitalism, subject to its economic laws, linked to it by something like an umbilical cord: "No slave society in modern times could free itself totally from the economic, social and moral influence of modern capitalism . . . an omnipresent rival buried deep within its economy and ideology and simultaneously confronting it from without." [15] The West Indian world was too small to successfully resist capitalist pressure. The first stroke came from navigation laws: Richard S. Dunn and Richard B. Sheridan have observed correctly that although the "glorious revolution" saved the planter class from the devastating effects of the Stuart economic policy, it nevertheless left them curbed and on the defensive. They more and more deserted their islands in order to go to London to spend their money peacefully and to defend their interests. There, they disappeared as a class and were individually absorbed by new conservative English groups. The unhealthy climate of the West Indies drove away more. The tremendous insurrection of Santo Domingo scared away others and, in the meantime, delivered the death blow to the French West Indian planter class. During the first decades of the nineteenth century the old slave societies of the West Indies were only relics of a dead era. The new industrial bourgeoisie, born of the industrial revolution, needed them no more: the era of mercantile capitalism had vanished. What English industries needed now were markets to absorb their tremendous output. Slavery now stood in their way as a stumbling block. It had to be abolished; and it was, even if the debris of the planter class survived it.

The case of Brazil was far different from that of the West Indies. The growth of the Brazilian seigneurial society had followed the same steps observed in any similar one. Slavery was introduced *en masse*, in the middle of the sixteenth century, when Brazil first began to supply the greed for sugar of European merchants.[16] So rose the *senhor de engenho*, so similar, as Gilberto Freyre [17] observed, to Virginia's, South Carolina's, or the West Indies' planters: ". . . the so-called 'deep South,' a region where a patriarchal economy created almost the same type of aristocrat and of the Big House, almost the same type of slave and of slave quarters, as in the north of Brazil." [18] The Brazilian *casa grande* was special in itself. "The Big House, although associated particularly with the sugar plantation and the patriarchal life of the northeast, is not to be looked upon as exclusively the result of sugar-raising, but rather as the effect of a slaveholding and latifundiary monoculture in general. In the south it was created by coffee, in the north by sugar. . . ." [19] Throughout the "tropical civilization," the *casa grande* unconsciously followed the Brazilian patterns, casting them into the individual style of local cultures.

There the Brazilian planter lived as a patriarch, being to his big "family" everything short of God: master, mentor, banker, administrator, tyrant, father (frequently in the literal sense of the word). At its best, life there was calm and harmonious, lavish and luxurious, founded on the rhythm of agriculture. The medieval system of "open house" was usual among Brazilian planters, as well as wasteful economics. Indeed, Brazilian planters lived so luxuriously as to cause foreigners to wonder; they should have wondered, too, had they any chance to check the accounts of such families, which were weighed down with debts. As Caio Prado said, latifundia, monoculture, and slave labor had, as results, debts.[20] The Brazilian, as well as the Caribbean and southern, economy was completely dependent on international banks; linked to capitalism, it actually was dependent on it.

Seigneurial planters, however, always maintained intellectual hegemony. Among the most striking examples in the Old South is that of the Jones family from New England. Of good Puritan origin, once established in Liberty County, Georgia, they quickly acquired a completely southern, slaveholding, seigneurial mind, and consequently had several members who fought bitterly and valiantly in the Civil War.[21] In the same way Brazilian planters all but absorbed the Dutch who remained in Brazil after their defeat. Those Dutch represented—in Brazil—albeit for a short period, the tentative introduction of a system based on industry and trade, against which rural Brazilian patriarchs reacted after the Dutch had been swept away.

As in the Caribbean, Brazilian cuisine was sophisticated and rich in Afro-American recipes. Still alive, it boasts such dishes as acarà, caruru, tomugunzà, and xinxim.[22] It is interesting to note that in Louisiana the name "gumbo" comes from the West-African word "ngombo."

Both in colonial and imperial Brazil, the *senhores* kept power strictly under their control: theirs were the most important positions both in the army and in public administration. However, characteristically, their participation in public life increased when, charged with debts, unable to keep abreast of growing industrial prices, their class began to crumble. As in the Old South and in the West Indies, the slave system was wasteful, it exhausted the land, so that it bore within itself the causes of its dissolution. Slavery in Brazil survived the American Civil War: it took a long time to die. When the bourgeois groups, who wanted to foster European immigration, pushed through anti-slavery laws, immigration began to grow. It now appeared clear how much cheaper it was to exploit wage labor. This gave strong momentum to the abolition movement: slavery simply could not compete with the new machine age.[23]

Curiously, the best example of something similar is to be found very far from Brazil, in South Carolina. There, the big rice dynasties and their great land properties began to crumble after the Civil War. The soft, muddy soil prevented the utilization of machinery: for this reason, rice culture was doomed. Its collapse brought with it the collapse of the old aristocratic planter class: the "Carolina Rice Plantation Society" of today has no Carolinian in it. The only rice still cultivated in South Carolina is a very small amount, grown mainly to attract ducks! [24]

The Spanish-American hacienda, with or without slavery,

closely followed the patterns already noted in French-Canadian manors, West-Indian plantations, and Brazilian seigneurial properties. "The hacienda," wrote Frank Tannenbaum, "is not just an agricultural property owned by an individual. The hacienda is a society, under private auspices. It is an entire social system and governs the life of those attached to it from the cradle to the grave. It encompasses economics, politics, education, social activities, and industrial development." [25]

Everybody familiar with Old South or West Indies plantations will find here striking similarities between the hacienda and the plantation. But on plantations (as on slaveholding haciendas) slaves were far more linked "from the cradle to the grave" to their master than peons were to theirs.

Tannenbaum even pointed out that the domestic economy of haciendas, where everything was manufactured on the property, was the same as on southern plantations of the eighteenth century. This habit went on, in the Old South, until the downfall of the slave system, as far as common products were concerned. However, the nearness of a great industrial region and the pressure, both economic and psychological, exerted by such a region upon the South foretold the death of self-sufficiency. In addition, the worsening colonial status of the South, which more and more put both the marketing and shipping of cotton abroad into the hands of northern bankers, brokers, businessmen, traders, and skippers, facilitating the sale of northern products in the South, opened the way, in a limited sense, to the introduction of "extraneous" manufactured goods. The plantation remained, however, a very limited market. The richest planters bought items for their own consumption and coarse clothes for slaves, but foodstuffs and everyday implements, tools, furniture, and garments were still locally produced. (How could one forget the "homespun," which was the basic fabric for the garments of small southern planters and yeomen, the poor, and the blacks, and even planters on routine days?) The South, owing to slavery, remained a relatively closed economy, or, better, a complex of closed economies, with a very poor, almost nonexistent market.[26]

In the Old South, as in the West Indies, Brazil, and Spanish America, urban life was limited.[27] The center of activity was elsewhere, in the "big houses" among plantation fields. There great planters lived, like true seigneurs, frequently even enjoying privileges of a feudal nature, like the Brazilian planters, whose property by law could not be expropriated in case of debts.[28] Land was their strength, their life, their philosophy. "Southern colonists," wrote C. Vann Woodward, "established plantations, not cities; and cultivated staples, not trade." [29] The same may be said of both Brazil and Canada; so that the South turned out to be more akin to distant Brazil and far-off Canada than to New England or New York.

From its very beginnings, the paternalistic planter class had set precise ideals and aims for its life. Their culture, wrote Gilberto Freyre, was "characterized more by the desire . . . to enjoy life—through the appreciation of a well-cooked fish, a good cigar, fine guitar music, and kindness and tolerance to others—than by the pursuit of material gains or highly intellectual conquests that might prove detrimental to a slow and pleasant rhythm of existence." [30] This was, of course, Brazil: however, all over the seigneurial world of the Americas it was certainly true that this civilization was absolutely free from the puritan idea of leisure as a sin. Brazilian planters distinguished themselves by lavish, princely hospitality, luxurious garments, tables furnished with silver.[31] The Old South was by no means different. When the revivalist preacher George Whitefield arrived in Charleston, South Carolina, in the first half of the eighteenth century, he found those people "wholly devoted to pleasure, polite entertainment, dancing masters . . . and the sin of wearing jewels." [32] The old Italian Renaissance tradition had taken very deep root, indeed!

All this, in fact, came together with an exquisite and refined culture. Writing to a friend, Eliza Lucas Pinckney informed her correspondent that she was able to sing French songs, having taken "some pains" to keep her French; [33] the same lady used to receive fine clothes from England, sent at great expense. Throughout the colonial Americas (usually considered a wilderness by contemporary Europeans), the planter classes boasted a very high standard of sophisticated culture: they spoke French, Italian, and other languages; [34] kept good libraries where Latin and Greek authors were to be found; [35] and sent their children to study in Europe.[36]

The plantation, as already stressed, was not only a producing unit: it was far more, a world in itself. When the civilization of the Old South emerged, the Brazilian and West Indian cultures were already old, rich, and opulent. The eighteenth century's Brazilian planters had already begun to use middlemen for marketing their products; an analogous figure, the so-called factor, rose in the Old South at the beginning of the cotton era. But the pattern was the same.

In this civilization, members of the seigneurial classes grew paternalistic, arrogant, lazy, slow; however, the basic military character of such a civilization (as of any precapitalist culture, where the hero has always been the soldier, the warrior, not the moneymaker) came to the fore when they had to fight desperately against heavy odds to drive away from Brazil French and English interlopers, Dutch invaders, and fierce Indian nations; [37] and one has only to recall how southern planters rose fiercely to fight the North in the War for Independence. It is, however, very important to underline the fact that Brazilian planters fought capitalist Holland when their seigneurial regime was still in the prime of life, whereas southerners had to fight northern industrial capitalism at the maximum of its tremendous power.

Relations other than productive linked masters and slaves. First, a conspicuous number of blacks were removed from productive duties and switched to the unproductive tasks of attending their masters' houses and families. Among these people, it has been demonstrated, a true spirit of caste arose, insulating them from the "despised" field hands, considered to be "inferior," and binding them to a kind of intimacy and solidarity with the "family." Truly, they were, in a sense, members of the family. The basic difference between the patriarchal, seigneurial "big family" and the cellular, monogamic family of today cannot be stressed enough. Slaves really were members of the "family," as in a primitive, tribal organization;

one has to go back to biblical times to find something like it. Such aspects of slavery very easily dispose of the absurd pretense that it was "a kind of capitalism." Where there is no wage labor, there is no capitalism.[38] Miscegenation was the immediate consequence of such a social organism. For a long time, miscegenation in the southern United States was carefully minimized, avoided, and concealed even by historians; it existed, nevertheless, as more recent scholars have definitely demonstrated.[39]

So, in the late eighteenth century, seigneurial America was flourishing, from Brazil to Canada. However, this civilization was fast nearing sunset. The world by now was very different from the era of Columbus, Verrazzano, even of Ralegh. All over the world, the old ruling classes were being routed by the bourgeoisie. Under the impulse of New England, Great Britain (now under bourgeois rule) had delivered the death blow to *la Nouvelle France*, the first seigneurial society to be toppled. The consequences were not exactly those looked for by New Englanders. Louisiana went to Spain, later to return after American independence to join the other slaveholding states; Canada was not given to the colonists, but kept under royal rule, so that something of the old French civilization might survive. Spain was crumbling and unable to resist the onslaught of other powers; Portugal, since the Methuen Treaty, had become an English colony except in name. Consequently, Latin America's seigneurial societies lay open to English capitalist penetration: no Salvador de Sa was any longer there to repel the intruders. Only in the future would British capitalists be challenged in Latin America—by North American capitalists.

6

The Impact of the Industrial Revolution

If we try to picture a comprehensive landscape of old southern civilization from the very moment when the first European explorer, intoxicated with the classic spirit of the Italian Renaissance, reached its shores, to its apex, when the civilization succeeded in expressing its own "ideal state" as the Confederate States of America, we certainly see the nineteenth century as the climax of it, albeit not because of cotton. Cotton, indeed, was a contingent element, brought to the South by forces the South could not and did not control and imposed, so to speak, on the South by the fast-proceeding industrial revolution in modern technological countries by means of the despotic rule of the capitalist world market. So the South was dragged into the whirlpool of this protean market, there to find the illusion of a heretofore unknown kind of prosperity. It was a prosperity generated only by a special and temporary conjuncture in an industrial world totally extraneous to the South itself.

At the very moment the South was reaching what seemed the height of a favorable economic situation, it was in fact becoming more dependent, more subject to storms from far-off industrial countries, more exploited by the North. Every contradiction concealed inside its backward precapitalist system was exploding, culminating in the final explosion that annihilated this old-fashioned world.

Up to the eighteenth century, the South had enjoyed favorable relations with the capitalist world market. It produced tobacco, rice, and indigo, and marketed them by means of "British merchants who sold the crops, purchased and shipped manufactured goods and advanced credit when required." [1] This was the oldest way of selling southern products. However, well before the American Revolution, British merchants were gradually replaced by local people, frequently clerks from old English firms, who took over the tasks of storage, sale, and shipping. Such was the origin of the already mentioned "factors," those middlemen who, in the nineteenth century, did the same with southern cotton. However, in the seventeenth and eighteenth centuries, worldwide capitalism had not yet entered the industrial revolution; its capacity for absorbing colonial products and transforming them into manufactured goods was still limited. For this reason, precapitalist seigneurial societies could live rather comfortably near the fast-developing capitalist class.

The industrial revolution was to change the situation of the world market totally. During the era of so-called mercantile capital, it was precisely the limitation of the world market that allowed this kind of capital to prosper: as Maurice Dobb correctly observed, merchant capital was, consequently, in a sense, a parasite of the old order.[2] However, in a relatively short period, both the American and the French revolutions were fought. While glamorous revolutionary clashes resounded on the battlefields, other confrontations, more silent, were, as Marx observed, being fought in Great Britain: the battles of the industrial revolution. The industrial revolution spelled the doom for old-fashioned, mercantile bourgeois classes, giving the industrial bourgeoisie a tremendous expansive strength; trade became less important than production; the old colonial system, intended to exploit colonies in a mercantilist way, was fast nearing its end. Colonies had to be linked more and more to a single-staple system; the staple had to be the one necessary to industry in a given moment. But, more about this later.

With the coming of the industrial revolution, manufacturing production skyrocketed. Carlo M. Cipolla underlined that, until the industrial revolution, "animal and vegetal worlds furnished the biggest part of energy needed by mankind in order to live, procreate, and produce. . . . The industrial revolution opened the door to a completely new world based upon incredible sources of energy, coal, oil, electricity, atom, all exploited by means of engines. . . ." [3]

What usually is not well understood is the fact that even during the preindustrial era, mankind already possessed many factories that produced and sold manufactured goods, frequently of exquisite workmanship, albeit more artisan than industrial. Mankind even had mines, extracted iron, coal, copper, and tin. However, such industrial and mining activity was almost totally subordinated to agriculture. Not only was the ruling class almost completely agrarian (and the political class was, in turn, recruited from members of the agrarian class), but the great majority of people worked in agriculture; and the annual increase of per capita income did not average more than 1.5 percent yearly.

The industrial revolution changed everything. Agricultural production became more and more subordinated to industrial activity; in the past (as is still true in the Old South) factories and mines had the task of producing whatever goods were required by the increase of agricultural production. Now, agriculture was more and more called upon to produce what was necessary to the development of industry. And industry wanted cotton, cotton, cotton, in incredible quantities. In this way, the first impact of the industrial revolution on the Old South was its transformation into the cotton kingdom.

A few decades later, something similar happened in Brazil, where, under the pressure of the demand of distant markets, the whole Paraíba Valley became the "coffee country" and soon experienced a boom as incredible as had been the cotton boom of the South. When the world market became clogged and no longer needed Brazilian coffee in such immense proportions,[4] the prosperity of the coffee country, of course, collapsed.

Then, one more step was taken. Growing more and more powerful, needing wider and wider markets, more capital to invest, greater masses of "free" wage labor, capitalism could no longer coexist with old-fashioned, backward societies. Indian nabobs, Chinese mandarins, African kings, and southern and Latin-American planters had now to yield whatever power they still had, thus reducing themselves to a secondary role in the framework of the new capitalist world.

The most serious and ominous difference that was growing between the two societies, a difference missed by many scholars too fascinated by numbers, was ideological. A social class like the modern industrial bourgeoisie, which had come to power through revolutions, could no longer reconcile itself with "the world the slaveholders made." The new scale of values of a class that had defeated in Europe the old-fashioned aristocracies and feudal or quasi-feudal monarchies could no longer accept the "shame and the sin" of a slave society. As Eric Foner justly points out, the new watchword was soon to become "free soil, free labor, free men." Free soil meant the breakdown of the old plantation system, which had to be limited to what already existed, waiting to be "suffocated like a rat in a hole"; free labor meant to "free" the slave laborers from plantations in order to send them into the great "industrial reserve army" of the unemployed, assuring in this way cheap labor for the new industrialism; free men meant the extension to everybody of the bourgeois idea of freedom, for better and for worse.

So it was that, initially, the "coffee revolution" had come to Brazil and the "cotton revolution" to the South; however, as Brazil was far beyond the industrial pale, its slaveholding society was allowed to exist for some time more; but the northern United States' bourgeoisie, at least from 1850, could no longer tolerate the "cancer" of the slave South inside its borders. The true problem was to give birth to a unified national market, achieved through the complete unification of America, and the possible creation of an American nation, as had just been done in Italy and was soon to be done in Germany.

Italy had been the test case. Was it possible to go ahead with two different economic systems, one in the North, the other in the South? Unlike the United States, northern Italy was a free-trade country, whereas southern Italy had a protective tariff. The first act of the new unified Italian government was to eliminate the tariff, thus destroying in a few months whatever industry had begun to rise in the South. Southerners, it was alleged, did not need industry; they could migrate north to find jobs—for very low wages, obviously. So they, labeled with the scornful and insulting name of *terroni*, began to migrate northward, there to live in huge, filthy urban ghettos.

Shortly after the unification of Italy, the United States entered the secession crisis: the bell was tolling for another pre-capitalist society, the slave South. The industrial revolution moved ahead at a very quick step. The northern United States had reached the arena of the industrial revolution rather late, after Great Britain, even after France. At this point, industry claimed protective tariffs, in order to deny the dreaded entry of both English and French manufactured goods. The industrial revolution was turning to the light another part of its hidden face: the need for capital, on a hitherto unseen scale. Where had English industry found the capital required by the needs of its primary accumulation? By expropriating and destroying the domestic yeomen and turning abroad for raw agricultural products. In other words, in the era of the industrial revolution, agriculture had not only to go on producing whatever staple was required by industry, it had even to finance the industrial revolution by yielding, whether it liked it or not, a large part of its income.

As we have seen, immediately after Italian unification in 1861, the first step of the northern industrial bourgeoisie, which now governed the country, had been the complete abolition of protective tariffs in order to raze whatever industry the agrarian South possessed. This done, a few years later the Italian government reintroduced higher and higher tariffs, in order to compel the agricultural areas (mainly the South) to buy northern industrial products—poorly made and more expensive —instead of better and cheaper foreign products.[5] Very soon, whatever economic activity survived in the Italian South fell under the control of large northern banks. It should be noted that another aspect of the industrial revolution is the tremendous expansion of large banks linked to industrial capital; they fast superseded the old, relatively small banks, which had formerly provided limited-scale land credit.

The same thing was happening in the United States. During the "good old times," southern factors had been linked to London's or Liverpool's trading firms; now they were becoming more and more dependent on large northern banks. Northern banks made the loans that financed the marketing and sale of southern cotton, shipped from America aboard northern ships. While it is true, as Fogel and Engerman [6] stress, that southern planters netted handsome profits by selling cotton, the fact is that such profits rested very briefly in southern pockets and soon found their way north to defray the enormous debts contracted with northern banks. Incidentally, it might be worth studying the role of such banking groups, which did not want to strangle the hen laying the golden eggs, in resisting the eventual confrontation. However it may be, the more the cotton "boom" increased, the more the South was becoming dependent, colonial, and exploited.[7]

But northern industry now wanted and needed more—more markets, more labor. As a market for northern goods, the South was narrow, poor, and almost useless; as a source of labor, it counted for nothing. Slavery kept "frozen" a tremendous labor force that should have been made "free"; it gave support to a planter oligarchy that wielded considerable power and might even try to escape the suffocating pressure from the North by increasing its economic relations with Great Britain and France. The South did in fact do so, heavily damaging the industrial development of the North. The time was nearing to pass from an economic to a political hegemony of the North over the South; the time was coming for testing the issue of "one nation or two." Moreover, the basic industrial capitalist ideology of the North was fast becoming nationalistic, liberal, and equalitarian (certainly, within the frame of a bourgeois society).[8] Everything in the Old South, its aristocratic and oligarchic society, its backward social organization, its old-fashioned and "barbarous" institution of slavery, its pretense of constituting a separate national entity, was fast becoming loathsome to the North.[9]

In the meantime, the South was basking in the sun of possibly its best period since its birth. Cotton was king; it was sold all over the world. In spite of the appalling debts that plagued the South, its profits were big enough to afford a standard of life better than ever before; moreover, the old southern civilization was now mature enough, old enough, to have reached the maximum possible degree of self-consciousness, of intellectual and social understanding. Looked at from our era, the old southern civilization between 1830 and 1860 shines with a mild and gentle light that is only attained by civilizations on the very edge of collapse and disintegration.

Soon the South would have just one path to follow: to reach its end by trying to build up what is the highest product of any civilization, its "ideal state," the living embodiment of its philosophy. Like any other "ideal state," the southern Confederacy was destined to be utopian, doomed to defeat, albeit to a magnificent defeat, its ideal heritage to be handed down to following generations to meditate upon. The fact that we are frequently unable to understand its message results from the fact that we, too, are children of a modern, liberal, and industrial civilization, so that we allow a kind of moralistic judgment to creep invisibly inside our minds to warp what should be only a purely historical evaluation.

That the South, as a whole, had reached the maximum of self-consciousness is clearly revealed by its belief, more and more clearly held, that it should be a "separate nation." Now, the idea of nation is no "eternal and hypostatic" category; it does not exist in itself, separately from material conditions. No Italian or German nation ever existed before having reached the mature self-consciousness of being one; a nation is generated gradually by its own progressive self-consciousness, insofar as this spreads more and more through members of such a "nation." It is obvious that the national idea that may appear from time to time in some insulated intellectuals does not mean, in itself, that such a nation is already born; the Italian nation did not begin to be born when Dante or Machiavelli had some idea of it, but when such an idea became widespread.

The idea of a southern nation was, in part, generated by contrast. The outside world, since entering, at the end of the eighteenth century, the industrial revolutionary era, was fast changing; the Old South was immobile in its social and economic structures. The gap was widening. So, strange as it may seem, southern nationalism was generated not by progress, but by conservatism. However, this was by no means an isolated case: Irish, Polish, and Indian nationalism, at least in the mid-nineteenth century, were much the same. Incidentally, they all were ideologies of old-fashioned agrarian nations, which, at least in the cases of Ireland and India, were resisting a highly industrialized, modern, liberal society. Nationalism is not necessarily liberal and "progressive": the defense of traditions may be equally, if not more, important, as may be the case of defending one's soul.

So we are back to this point: the most dramatic contrast between the South and the North was neither economic nor moralistic: in fact, it was ideological. At its heart, it was still the sharp contrast between an Elizabethan, classically minded, aristocratically individualistic South and a puritanical, trade-minded, Calvinistic North.

Puritanism, as we have stressed, had been the master ideology for a capitalist society; now, looking beneath the surface, all its values were enhanced. Certainly, men like Emerson boasted of being freethinking, liberal-minded laymen; apparently, they had nothing to do with bigoted puritan priests. However, a close scrutiny of their ideologies would show the puritan scale of values still deeply buried in their souls. Ideological intolerance *vis-à-vis* different social organization, no more, to be sure, condemned as sinful, but as "illiberal," "obscurantist," "barbarous"; division of mankind no more between "saints" and "devils," but between "progressives" and "reactionaries." Upon this followed ideological excommunications, political and economic liberalism (free enterprise, free labor), consideration of profit no longer as a concession from God, but as the proper economic reward of "a right economic

62

system," and so on. Their utter incapability of understanding what other societies were like; their pretense of "civilizing" them and compelling them, by brute force if necessary, to adopt the "correct" economic and social system; their branding of slaveholders as "brutes, criminals, sinners," were nothing else than old Puritanism in new, "liberal" clothes.

Southern Civilization at Its Peak

Whereas the North was following such puritan ideologies, the southern ruling class was still sticking to its classical Renaissance origins. Classicism had, in the South of the late eighteenth and nineteenth centuries, a splendid revival.[1] When Georgia decided to establish its university, the hill where it was to be built was christened "Athens": there the sons of planter aristocracy were to go to study the humanities, Latin, history. Immediately thereafter, a series of such institutions—completely state-sponsored and free from any religious affiliation—spread all over the South.

So high was the consciousness of cultivated southerners as learned representatives of classic culture, that John Randolph of Roanoke contemptuously said that he had never seen "a yankee who knew anything about the classics." And the bare fact that a most hated northern politician, William Henry Seward, rejected anything Roman as an example worthy of imitation by America made Southerners even more proud of their classic heritage. Higher education in the South was rarely pursued without a deep study of Latin and Greek; classic culture (it was openly said) was what distinguished a true gentleman.[2] George Fitzhugh underlined the similarity between his own ideas and

Aristotle's, and, even more, between Aristotle's and John C. Calhoun's.

Indeed, the oratory of the great South Carolinian was classically severe, more akin to Latin tradition than to an Anglo-Saxon heritage. It was observed that Calhoun's presence in the United States Senate "reminded friend and foe alike of a Senator of Rome"; [3] and Lewis Cass was perhaps right when he nicknamed Calhoun *Ultimus Romanorum*. Calhoun had made a deep study of the Roman Constitution. There, in the Tribuni's veto, he thought he had found the democratic device to keep the Union together; from it he worked out his idea of a "concurrent majority."

However, as already observed, southern thought was more and more turning toward Greece, instead of Rome, as an ideal example. Southerners were pleased with the Greek system of small-scale states and with Greek local autonomies. Certainly, they deeply resented the appellation that Bostonians were giving to their city: "the Athens of America" (indeed, a not-at-all deserved one). Perhaps, southerners seemed to observe, Massachusetts was akin to Athens only because its trials of witches might somewhat resemble Athens' trial of Socrates!

Southerners liked to make comparisons of their individual states with Laconia, Attica, Arcadia, and so on. Perhaps the apex was to be reached after war and defeat, when an exquisite classical scholar, who had been an officer in the Confederate service, Basil A. Gildersleeve, wrote a small book, a true last will of the ideal southern world, entitling it *A Southerner in the Peloponnesian War*.[4]

Culture, classic and humanistic culture, always loomed large in the southern aristocracy. It represented a true means of fulfillment, an individual and social achievement in itself. Planters were proud of attending classical schools. On December 22, 1860, the very moment when the United States was on the edge of being drawn into the whirlpool of secession and war, Robert Allston, a great rice planter of South Carolina, a refined lover of fine arts, received a letter from his son, Charles, in which he discussed at length Plutarch's *Lives*, which he was then reading.[5] This interest was well in line with family traditions. One of his family's most prominent members, Robert himself was a deeply cultivated and widely traveled man who liked to write verses on classic and heroic subjects, such as a poem on Hannibal, "the Carthaginian hero." [6] His accounts of travels in Europe still make for delightful reading.

Plutarch's *Lives* was a favorite book among planters. Mary Ann Lamar, sister of a prominent Georgia planter and wife of Howell Cobb, read it frequently and her knowledge was more than casual.[7] Her brother, John Basil Lamar of Milledgeville, Georgia, was another very cultivated and refined man, who liked to live "in the quiet enjoyment of a large fortune, of foreign travel, the gratification of elegant and literary tastes." [8] Writing to his sister, he once said he was sitting at an old table "covered by the most classic confusion of volumes of Shakespeare, History of Greece and Decline of Roman Empire. . . ." [9]

But the most symbolic episode, revealing the deep roots of the classic mentality, was perhaps to be found once again in the Allston "dynasty." Adele Allston, wife of Robert Allston, writing to her son Charles, who was far from home in the Confederate Army fighting the War for Independence, showed it in a clear, almost dramatic way. It was April 1862; in the West, the bloody battle of Shiloh had just been fought; Farragut was ready to enter the Mississippi and take New Orleans; in Virginia, McClellan was nearing Yorktown, there to advance on Richmond; from the Sea Islands, the federals were threatening the very hearts of South Carolina and Georgia, and the sound of their guns may have been heard in the Allston family "big house." In such a tragic moment, in the midst of the very nightmare of war, Adele Allston strove to ensure that her son would not become only a man who-killed-not-to-be-killed. She (like Boethius in his death cell) remembered the *Consolatione Philosophiae*, how much spiritual life and culture may help a sensible soul to wade across the miseries of life at war. So, she exhorted her son to learn the ancient Greek language, explaining to him the marvelous aspects of that unperishable civilization. It was a moving but chilling letter; these members of the old southern civilization *knew* (even if they did not dare to confess it, not even to themselves), or they at least *felt*, in the depth of their unconscious, that their civilization, their whole world, their way of life, their class, all was doomed. In such a moment they felt the need to go back to their beloved classical world, which, if long since dead as a body, was still alive as a soul, still able to speak to them, still sending through innumerable ages its mild, warm light, to encourage them and give them comfort.[10]

Planters liked well-furnished libraries, this is certain, but nowhere was their classical culture more evident than in southern architecture. Their mansions struck the northern traveler immediately with "something of Baronial grandeur." [11] Indeed, for any agricultural civilization, the country mansion was of great importance; it was the cultural pivot of their world. Since the very beginning of the Old South, everything in the "big house," as in the hacienda, had been homemade, "from cutting down the pine trees to hanging the window blinds." [12] The "big house," however, had attained its most magnificent—classical—style when southern civilization had reached its maturity. In Europe, the destiny of classic style had been strange indeed. Splendid and beautiful in Palladio's villas (which answered to the real intellectual need of a vanishing agrarian aristocracy), it had been cool and artificial in Napoleon's era. The truth was that the social structure which in Europe had given birth to Palladian classicism was long since dead. Surely, the new Napoleonic bourgeoisie liked to dress itself in classic garments; however, this was only a masquerade, exactly as Napoleonic "aristocracy" was false.

But in the Old South classicism was congenial with another true agrarian aristocracy. In Thomas Jefferson's era it was rediscovering its ideal linkings with "Roman" style through the eighteenth century Enlightenment (which, in itself, was a legitimate son of the Italian Renaissance). Enlightenment's classicism found a congenial habitat in the southern aristocratic mind, which, after all, descended from Elizabethan Renaissance classicism. The rediscovery of Palladian architecture is a chapter in itself in Jefferson's intellectual biography. In the beginning, the ideal tie was with republican Rome. But later, when southerners were being cornered and becoming conscious of being a minority, Roman ideals gave way—even in architecture—to Greek models.

At the same time another change was taking place. Southern aristocracy was beginning to spend more and more of its time in the small cities of the Old South. As in Brazil, in the South the seventeenth century had been mainly an era of isolated country houses; this situation went on, in part, during the early decades of the eighteenth century. In that period some of the most beautiful aristocratic mansions were built, either in the "Peninsula" of Virginia or in lower South Carolina, from Shirley to Carter's Grove to Hampton, although South Carolina would soon boast a "major" city, Charleston (which, in the beginning, was mainly a seaport with warehouses and trade buildings). Then, a noticeable shifting toward cities began. This era witnessed the building of fine houses on Charleston's Battery. At the same time, to the south, Brazilian owners of large plantations were shifting from old-fashioned, country *casas grandes* toward urban *sobrados*, which, strange to say, were characterized by great verandas, similar to Charleston's famous "piazzas" and intended to permit, even inside towns, some life *en plein air*.[13] Beautiful, unforgettable small cities were then growing or rising: Charleston and Georgetown, South Carolina; new residential areas in Richmond, Virginia; and several others, south through Georgia, Alabama, and Mississippi, to the very shores of the "Father of Waters."

This kind of urbanization was, however, *sui generis*. There is a remarkable difference between cities in agrarian civilizations and cities in industrial areas. In the first case, the center of production was in the country; cities were only places for aristocrats to meet (how to forget, here, the splendid, fascinating Meeting Street, in Charleston, South Carolina, true seigneurial *boudoir*?), to give parties, to exchange ideas, to go to balls, theaters, etc. Cities, in such civilizations, were not places where income was produced, but places where it was consumed. This should not be construed to mean that such cities had no artisans or manufacturers; they, indeed, had several. But their first and foremost economic activity was not in itself enough to characterize them as industrial cities. Except for the famous Tredegar Iron Works of Richmond, Virginia, factories in southern cities were small; even Tredegar was small in comparison with factories in the North. In the second place, many a manufacturer was also (and mainly) a planter, and his manufacturing activity was subordinated to his agrarian interests. Thirdly, the planter class showed a remarkable tendency to absorb persons from different activities. In the eighteenth century, merchants like Robert Pringle and Henry Laurens turned planters well before the ends of their lives.[14] In this way the planter class showed its hegemony and also asserted the real essence of its society. James Hammond saw this very clearly and stated it outspokenly.[15]

As Brazilian planters did when they passed from *casas grandes* to urban *sobrados*, southern planters, too, gave their city mansions a distinctly agrarian character, by means of gardens, trees, etc. Something like this is still to be seen in Italian Renaissance cities, which developed when rural aristocrats went to live in them for political reasons. A number of delightful cities (like Ferrara, Mantova, Urbino, Cortona, Città di Castello) still preserve such charming features: everywhere, concealed by walls, are small or large gardens, clumps of trees, even kitchen gardens, which contribute to city life a rural character, like the deep roots that still link those cities to their agricultural background, the real source of their wealth and power.

In the South the era of the cities was doomed to be brief, of course; and the Old South had no large cities, except New Orleans, and by 1860, it was already well into its decline. As far as customary urban life is concerned, southern cities had very little of it. Plantations were self-sufficient, and the population of towns was almost totally composed of planters and slaves. Eugene D. Genovese has stressed the fact that about 37 percent of the population in Mobile, Alabama, Savannah, Georgia, and Charleston, South Carolina, were either slaves or free blacks, with very little purchasing power. Because of this, urban markets for foodstuffs almost did not exist.[16] In other words, such centers, more than cities in the modern sense of the word, were agglomerates of rural mansions, with as much of industry and trade as suited the interests of the planters and mainly owned and controlled by the planters themselves. In the South the country still prevailed over the city and dominated it.

The country did not mean only the planters; it also meant the black slaves, who were the country laborers. The cultural influence of black Africans on the Old South is now, at last, being seriously studied. Such scholars as John W. Blassingame, George P. Rawick, and Orlando Patterson, among others (and, first among them all, Eugene D. Genovese), have stressed in a masterful way how a black culture not only existed and continued to develop under the almost prohibitive conditions of slavery, but also influenced widely and deeply the white culture, thus producing a complex southern culture in which original African elements are blended in an inextricable way, having fully disappeared as such in order to reemerge in a completely original and new blend.

It still remains to be studied more closely *how much* the characteristic culture of the seigneurial society was affected by the black culture. Such an inquiry will certainly demonstrate that the Afro-American contribution to the culture of the planter civilization was enormous. In the particular case of the Old South, its innermost culture was a very complex blend of the Italian classicism of the Renaissance (in large part through its derivation, Elizabethan classicism); the Spanish seigneurial system, from Ponce de León to Ayllón and the Georgia missions; [17] the French-American seigneurial system and culture through the Creole society of Louisiana; Amerindian culture, and African culture. All these elements cooperated to make the southern culture original and distinctive, more complex, spicy, and colorful than, for instance, the capitalist culture of the northern United States. It was less akin to the northern culture than to those of other plantation regions, which composed with the South the large and protean area of "tropical civilization." As Frank Tannenbaum wrote: "The institution of slavery had logic of its own. Wherever it existed in this hemisphere it worked its way into the social structure and modified the total society. The slave system was broader in its impact than might be discerned from a reading of the slave laws. The law itself was but evidence of the influence of slavery as an institution upon the *mores*. . . . Wherever we had slavery, we had a slave society, not merely for the blacks, but for the whites, not merely for the law, but for the family, not merely for the labor system, but for the culture—the total culture." [18]

Perhaps, among the several influences that molded the southern civilization, the most important (even if the least understood) was the black element. Prominent anthropologists have already begun to study both the rich essence of African cultures and the derived Afro-American culture; [19] I firmly believe that, in this field, historians will never be able to make serious progress without wide and deep interdisciplinary work with anthropologists. It will be necessary to study the individual links between the treasures of southern popular culture and the black heritage. For instance, an intriguing subject is the rich lode of southern popular proverbs and the wonderful wealth of proverbs of the Mande, from the African Gold Coast, the starting point of so many slaves on the infamous "middle passage." It will be necessary to discover the connections between the peculiar genius of the South for short stories and tall tales and of the Bété of West Africa for folktales.[20] As far as music is concerned, everybody acknowledges the basic, fundamental contribution to southern music (and not only to popular songs) of the Afro-American musical culture.[21]

But the African heritage inside the southern seigneurial culture is by far wider and deeper. It permeates many habits and ways of living, even in less obvious areas: a certain tendency toward good-humored leisure; styles of cooking; even accent. As far as the last is concerned, the African influence on southern English is becoming more and more the subject of study by philologists. They are in the process of tracing its influence as they have already done (at least, in part) with the French-Creole influence. The same study should be made of the Spanish language.

Perhaps the major consequence of the presence of black slaves was their effect on the image that planters began to form of themselves. It may be supposed that the slave idea of the paternal "Massa" helped the planter aristocracy to feel as they felt. This does not mean only that they were encouraged to look at themselves as naturally endowed with power, and, in some cases, to feel arrogant and overbearing, but refers to something less simple. Planters began to "individualize" themselves, to "understand" themselves from a peculiar standpoint, to live up to their "social function" of quasi-feudal seigneurs. It must be true that the serf makes the seigneur, at least as much as the seigneur makes the serf. African slaves, it must be stressed, "helped" planter aristocrats to think of themselves as "that particular kind of seigneur." The African civilizations from which the slaves came to America were all precapitalistic and agrarian, and any society of this kind is soundly based on patriarchalism, paternalism, and (in many cases) even true seigneurial classes with a strong hierarchical sense. African culture, therefore, would have played a prominent part in shaping the slaves' expectation of the kind of seigneurs they would find. Black slaves contributed in this way to giving the planter aristocracy its image of itself. After the destruction of slavery, planters with this mentality became "displaced persons" in the new context of a capitalist society that was totally extraneous to their "ethos." They would perhaps have felt more at ease among Algerian *caïds* or black African noblemen.

The relations master-to-slave and white-to-black were far more morbid, pathological, and twisted than they appear if taken only at face value. The dominant position of slaveholders was weakened by the fact that their intercourse with the slaves had a hidden side that always lay buried deep inside their unconscious and was never allowed to emerge to light.[22]

In the early nineteenth century, this patriarchal, paternalistic civilization was reaching its height. *Pari passu,* the sense of guilt was increasing inside the slaveholders' souls. Certainly, slavery was an evil (as is any exploitation); however, the justifications that the slaveholding class brought forth were not completely destitute of any foundation. It is true that, just before the Civil War era, southern slavery had reached possibly the most mild and humane (or least inhumane) level compatible with such a cruel institution. One is surprised to see planters (who should have been "shrewd businessmen") going directly against their economic interest, which they are supposed to have pursued like "able moneymakers," in order to respect the personality of their slaves. In 1835, John Basil Lamar, an important planter of Georgia, selling the slaves belonging to his father's unwilled property, purchased four of the old blacks and a deformed boy himself, because he thought they were unwilling to leave their old homes. Although they were no longer capable of any valuable work, he decided to disburse money in order to keep them with their relatives.[23] There were many cases like this on nineteenth-century plantations; and this certainly did not contribute, from a purely economic viewpoint, to making the plantations "very efficient" enterprises, as Fogel, Engerman, and their school allege them to have been.

There was no better witness of this situation than Charles Francis Adams, Jr. Answering a letter from his father, who, as was true of many northerners, mainly abolitionists, had a kind of contempt toward black slaves, the younger Adams wrote: "I'm getting to have very decided opinions on the negro question . . . I note what you say of the African race and 'the absence of all appearance of self-reliance in their own power' during this struggle. From this, greatly as it has disappointed me, I very unwillingly draw different conclusions from your own. The conviction is forcing itself upon me that African slavery, as it existed in our slave states, was indeed a patriarchal institution under which the slaves were not, as a whole, unhappy, cruelly treated or overworked. I am forced to this conclusion. Mind, I do not because of it like slavery any better. . . ." [24]

Very recently, a distinguished historian, Ludwell H. Johnson, reviewing the collection of the Jones family letters, and quoting an older one, the Fleet family letters collection, the first from Georgia, the second from Virginia, observed that those letters are "a compelling evidence" that the Old South, as depicted by writers like Thomas Nelson Page or Margaret Mitchell "did exist, that it is not the product of weak-minded romanticizing." [25] The same impression, I must add, is received by anybody going carefully and at length through the letters of many southern planter families.

All the vital elements coming from Africa blended, as already noted, with Elizabethan, Spanish, French, and even Italian aspects into southern culture. This rich background gave the planter class a consciousness of possessing a mentality of its own, which had almost nothing to do with the northern mentality. Perhaps, it should be stressed once more, it was more akin to other American cultures. I remember having been struck, when in Mexico City, by a new mural in the Hotel Colon, representing countries all around the Gulf of Mexico and the Caribbean. All these countries clearly represented parts of a sea-oriented world, their rivers running toward the same seas, and they turning, so to speak, their backs to the interior of the continent. All appeared characterized by very similar patterns of agrarian economies and cultures: the Old South, with its stately mansions, its cotton and rice fields, its towering steamboats moving like floating palaces down the Mississippi, its colorful quarters in Mobile and New Orleans; Mexico and Central America, with their haciendas, big houses, folkloristic dances, colorful cities; the sunburnt Caribbean islands, with their quasi-African folklore, lovely colonial cities, and large plantations producing sugar and coffee. This was, it seems, the world to which the Old South really belonged; and it is still to be discovered how much of this consciousness lay deep at the bottom of the so-called Southern dream of a Caribbean empire.[26]

Pondering the distinctive shape of mind of the seigneurial class of the South, one is irresistibly drawn into thinking of the agrarian "senatorial" class of the Roman Republic. The Romans were frequently good administrators, even shrewd "businessmen," as far as the development of their properties was concerned; however, to them, business was always *vile negotium*. What gave human life its taste and its meaning were the so-called *otia*, or cultural, literary, even scientific pursuits, entertaining lavishly, cultivating friendships. Here perhaps is to be found the key to understanding why and how southern gentlemen, however concerned about their business (and in many cases managing it very adroitly), never had a capitalist *Weltanschauung*. And this, incidentally, in the economic war to come, would represent their chief "inferiority" in comparison

74

to businessmen from the North. So one obtains the impression that money was to them only a means: the true aim of their lives was leisure, culture, and status. Increasing production was just a method to reach the true end: consumption.

Among the most important pursuits of the southern seigneurial class were military and political careers. A close scrutiny of the most prominent generals and officers in the Confederate army during the Civil War shows clearly that a military career was usually the choice of cadets from impoverished seigneurial families, very much as it was in the feudal noble class of Europe. Robert E. Lee is the most remarkable instance.[27] As far as politics is concerned, to understand the aristocrat-politicians of the Old South, it is necessary to dismiss any idea we may have of politicians from our own bourgeois world. The "professional" politician was scarcely, if ever, to be found in the Old South. In our bourgeois societies, politics may represent a career in itself, frequently a business. After all, in capitalist society everything has been transformed into a commodity, to be bought and sold, whose value is to be reckoned in terms of money. So, politics, too, has become a business. It is more and more an infrequent occurrence for politicians to retire at the end of their careers with less money than they had at the beginning, our social *ethos* being content to condemn only those who make money by "illicit" means. Members of parliaments receive appointments and, in many countries, very handsome ones. Certainly, this is a requirement of democracy, to allow even non-moneyed men to enter politics; but in many cases it may be a very deleterious source of corruption and bribery.

In the Old South, as in any aristocratic society, this was not usually the case. There were, of course, exceptions, but what matters here is the rule. Politicians were usually important planters with large estates. Studying their biographies closely, one gets the impression that they were not politicians at all, but planters who participated in politics. The South was no democratic society; it was an oligarchy, governed by a very intelligent, mild, shrewd, benevolent, and tolerant paternalistic class. However, poor whites very rarely became prominent politicians, and those who did fight their way up against the "plantocracy" succeeded only in jumping, in many cases, to "the other side of the river," as Andrew Johnson did.

As far as planters are concerned, one has only to peruse the papers of Thomas Jefferson, John Randolph, John C. Calhoun, Howell Cobb, Robert Toombs, and Jefferson Davis to see what kind of politicians they made. Ambitious they were—no man can go through life and accomplish anything without having a just ambition; but, climbers of the social ladder they almost never were. And what had they to climb for? They were already on the top, looking down from aloft on "inferior" classes. A remarkable member of the planter aristocracy, suggesting a social behavior to a younger member of the family, underlined that the best procedure was to be friendly to all but intimate with very few. The suggestion (a true Horatian *Odi profanum vulgus et arceo*) went to a lady, but gentlemen did not behave differently.[28]

Frequently, through political life, such planter-politicians lost money. Going to Washington, taking seriously their political duties, meant neglecting their plantations; frequently left in the hands of unreliable people, their planter's business went completely astray. In 1842, Howell Cobb of Georgia and his brother-in-law, John Basil Lamar, both prominent members of the seigneurial class, were nominated for Congress. Immediately John B. Lamar wrote Howell Cobb a letter in which, without even mentioning the real motives that prompted his resignation, in a *grand seigneur* way, he declared that he would not accept the nomination. Lamar wrote that he had wanted to show that he would not have passed "through the world as a perfectly obscure individual," but, having won the nomination, he did not care to be a politician.[29]

However, the real motives that prompted Lamar were deeper. He knew that his brother-in-law, a very generous and prodigal man, would soon have been completely bankrupt because of his plunging into politics. So Lamar, without breathing a word to his brother-in-law, decided that one politician in the family was enough; he would resign in order to dedicate himself completely to administering the estate and the interests of the family, so that his sister and his nephews would not starve and his brother-in-law would not be completely ruined. We know this only from his confidential letters, as Lamar was too generous and magnanimous, and even too proud, to confess to relatives what he was doing and why.[30]

Perhaps the most striking example of this mentality was Jefferson Davis. When he reached the required age, he entered, as a cadet, upon a military career, leaving the estate to his older brother. One is struck by the truly magnificent sacrifice; but what was most wonderful was the political career he entered afterward. He chose it, objectively, as the right thing to do; he duly resigned from service in the Mexican War; and when the Confederacy, at the Montgomery Convention, elected him its provisional President, he accepted against his will, as a duty. He did not want to become President; he saw in front of him a way with many thorns and very few roses, if any, but he would never have turned away from a duty. To do his duty was the substance of his life, and he did it, truly embodying the iron will of the South.[31] However criticized, abused, even slandered, he did not care to apologize or to give explanations. Why such an aloof and proud behavior? I believe that it was because he never considered politics as a career, but as a duty (or, better, as both a duty and a right for a man of his class).

A politician is, in a sense, an actor, whose audience is the whole world. So, like an actor, he has to care about what his audience thinks of him in the present, and what history will say of him in the future. Master politicians, like Napoleon, Cavour, and Lincoln, began very soon building up their legends and myths for the use of future generations. Augustus, on his deathbed, even asked rather cynically if he had played his part well. When answered in the affirmative, he said: "So, please, clap your hands, friends," and died. But Augustus was the most prominent member of a new, cynical, imperial class. Once again, southern seigneurs were very similar to members of the "senatorial" class of the Roman Republic, whose exponents were the Catos, not the Augustuses. Such men never had any idea of a political "career"; they simply considered politics as a duty—and an obvious right—of their class, like a great king who considered his duty that of being "the first servant of *his* people." That to rule was his right, he did not even bother to say—this was a matter of course.

I have frequently wondered about, among the most fascinating aspects of history, the rise of great political classes. The very idea of a "political class" sounds rather unfamiliar to our ears, and it does require some qualification.[32] In any given society, power is always in the hands of a ruling class (however challenged it may be). In the Old South, such a class was unquestionably that of the seigneurial planters. What characterizes any social class (either a ruling one, like the planters, or a subordinate one) is, usually, selfishness and a narrow-minded vision of immediate and egotistic economic interests. Certainly, such negative qualities can be more or less limited: a social class endowed by too narrow a mind cannot give birth to anything really great and lasting.

However, what is more important is the fact that any social class produces sooner or later an élite, which is what I call a "political class." Such a "political class" must be understood in a very wide and complex sense. For instance, in the Old South, it did not only include such men as Thomas Jefferson, John C. Calhoun, Jefferson Davis, and Howell Cobb, but also others, such as Edmund Ruffin, Henry Sidney Lanier, William Gillmore Simms, John Mercer Brooke, Edgar Allan Poe, and Matthew Fontaine Maury. Others might call it an "intellectual class." Or, as Gramsci wrote: "Any social group, having been born upon the original ground of a specific attribution in the sphere of economic production, gives birth, organically, to one or more intellectual classes which give it solidity and self-consciousness, not only as far as its economic activity is concerned: but even concerning the political one."[33] Others, drawing upon Gramsci, might use the term "intellectual class." I prefer to follow Giovanni Mosca and adopt the definition of "political class" in a wider sense. I understand that the word "intellectuals" might be more precise, but it is also likely to create more misunderstandings.

By what is a political class characterized? First, it constitutes, as already stressed, the "self-consciousness" of its ruling class as a whole. Secondly, its members distinguish themselves from other components of the social ruling class by their capacity for considering any problem on the highest possible level: the purely political one, without allowing any narrowly economic and egotistic residual consideration to intrude. This, in turn, means that members of the political class are capable of seeing not only the present interests of the social class they belong to but even the future concerns, so that they are able to "persuade" their social class to sacrifice present interests for future, and more valuable, objectives. Thirdly, they are capable of taking into consideration not only the limited and egotistic interests of the social class to which they belong, but even, and more, those of the dependent classes, so that they are able to "persuade" their social class to act as a defender of such subordinate interests. In this way the ruling class is transformed from a barely dominating group into a leading one, that is, able to rule not only by clumsy and brute force (which does not create any lasting or successful order), but, to a certain extent, by the consensus of subordinate groups. In other words, capable of exercising hegemony.

What matters here is that it can be reasonably maintained that the old southern civilization produced one of the most remarkable political classes in history. As Georg Weber wrote, "In their opinions and tendencies, they were inspired by an highmindedness superior to that of European aristocrats." [34] What was most admirable was the way in which they succeeded in understanding and interpreting the interests of the most dependent classes, even, in part, of black slaves. In a wonderful way they succeeded in giving to the slave subconscious a fair, lasting image of the "paternal master," making them feel like members of the "family" and, as a rule, treating them this way. Witness, for instance, a letter in which a planter, Mr. A. R. Wright, asked Howell Cobb to concede the hand of one of his slave girls to a black boy named Reuben, describing him as "honest, faithful and industrious." [35] They even succeeded in giving the slaves the ideal figure of the white planter as a kind of "social ideal," a true "ideal model." This is, perhaps, why, during the Civil War, the slaves never revolted, even when white women, children, and old people were almost completely in their hands—and any attempts from the North to raise such revolts were, in the main, dismal failures.

This character allowed members of the southern political élite to play a leading role in the government of the United States (at least until the rise of Free-Soilers) even when the South was more and more economically dependent. Certainly the slaveholders understood and felt such dependence. It may be argued that, beginning in 1820, the South was already fighting a purely rearguard battle. This may help to explain what is frequently dubbed the "*volte-face*" of John C. Calhoun. When the southern political class still believed it had the Union's government strongly in its hands (albeit by means of continuous compromises with the rising power of northern capitalism), Calhoun was a so-called nationalist; he even accepted moderate tariff duties as a token of a desired stronger alliance with the rising northern industrial class. However, that was not the kind of industry the South possessed: subordinated to agrarian interests or, at least, willing to compromise with such interests. Northern industrialists wanted power; and Calhoun, who had always been endowed with an icy-cool capability of seeing into the future, and with a deadly realism, understood very soon that the Old South was doomed. Only a rearguard fight might, perhaps, gain some time for discovering a new sort of compromise before the enemy's strength would make discussion impossible.

Accordingly, Calhoun proposed nullification first, and it failed. Then, in his 1850 speech, he advanced his more mature plan for allowing both sections to go on in passable terms and the Old South to survive. His plan aimed basically at transforming the Union into a kind of British Commonwealth, or into two Unions, linked forever by foreign policy and military defense but independent from each other on economic and social grounds. It is no wonder that his contemporaries did not in many cases understand the deep motivations that lay buried under Calhoun's so-called *volte-face*, when even present-day historians frequently fail to understand them. They go on

80

insisting on Calhoun's "opportunism," which is blatantly disproved by any careful study of Calhoun's papers.

Southerners felt more and more their fast worsening colonial status. John B. Lamar observed how indebted planters were,[36] and later, in 1849, told his brother-in-law, Howell Cobb, that the South, after paying the costs of subsistence for white planters and black slaves, turned the whole balance of its income over to the North to build cities, factories, ships, and palaces, and said without any circumlocution: "We occupy virtually the same relation to the Yankees that the Negroes do to us." [37]

Incidentally, this may be a response to the observations of Robert W. Fogel and S. Engerman that the cotton South "netted handsome profits." Yes, certainly. But where did those profits go? This is the question. It seems that they paused very briefly in southern pockets before finding their way north. It was like Menenius Agrippa's tale about the hands revolting against the stomach. Certainly, should the hands allow the stomach to starve, they would starve in turn; but it seems more difficult to prove that the hands do strengthen their body by feeding the stomach of somebody else. Clement Eaton rightly stressed that "the most striking characteristic of Southern economy was that although the colonial connection with England had been broken, a new colonialism arose with respect to Northern business." [38]

This dependency was obviously increased by the wastefulness of the southern economy. When somebody wonders how this was, since planters in most cases administered their properties carefully, even with a shrewd sense of business, he simply ignores the fact that the wastefulness lay not in men but was intrinsic to the system. It was intrinsic not to the system in absolute, but only in comparison with modern capitalism. For the most part, planters cared for their estates well; though one cannot miss the impression that this was not because they were "businessmen" or "money-makers" (as, in some cases at least, they actually were), but because it was *their* life, what gave their lives a meaning, a sense. For capitalists, business *is* life. It was different with plantations, because they (as Ulrich

Bonnel Phillips rightly observed) were, in fact, more: they were a life, a civilization, and a civilization based only in part (unlike capitalism) on business. So, in plantation civilization, money was not an end in itself, as in capitalist ethos; it was a means. Ends were very different and more complex.

Strange to say, as its crisis was advancing, the South was elaborating its social thought. Ideas already discussed by John Taylor of Caroline, by John C. Calhoun (even by Thomas Jefferson) now reached their ultimate shape in the writings of George Fitzhugh. Not that Fitzhugh's ideas were accepted all over the South; as a matter of fact, they were not; but Fitzhugh's *Sociology for the South* was in itself a symptom that the South was fast reaching a point of no return. Beyond it, there was only the supreme attempt to give flesh and bones to southern nationalism by creating the "ideal state" of the Old South.

8

The Old South and the New Industrial Warfare

The most definite refutation of the Fogel and Engerman thesis concerning the "efficient economy" of the Old South is, perhaps, the casual observation that those distinguished historians (or, as they prefer to be called, "cliometricians") are, in a sense, very similar to the man who went to visit the zoo and did not see the elephant—because it was too big.

Fogel and Engerman have undoubtedly reached many valuable conclusions about the South, but it seems surprising to see how they simply ignore the "big thing": the war. War is, of course, a very unpleasant problem to deal with, and historians frequently choose to ignore it, dedicating their attention to the more suitable "arts of peace." Certainly, studying the rise and high noon of a civilization may be more pleasant than scrutinizing the grueling spectacle of its downfall and destruction, but a study of its demise, albeit less tasty, may be far more revealing. Even military historians are not exempt from blame, as they frequently prefer to dedicate their attention to "glorious deeds," rather than rummage through dirt and blood. However, it is in the study of war that the ultimate meaning of military history is to be found, because war, among other things, is the showdown of a civilization, its "moment of truth."

The Old South went to war and was defeated. And it was defeated because its economy was not "efficient" enough; because it was not able to face on the battlefields a modern industrial community, which could not be defeated by sheer valor; because it lacked the economic and technological organization of its enemy; because slaves, who seem to some historians like "modern workers on an assembly line," could not be turned to assembling gun carriages or steam engines; because the "extremely efficient plantation economy" was totally inefficient in producing and transporting supplies for a country at war. In other words, the South was defeated because the southern productive system and southern labor, in spite of strenuous efforts, had almost nothing of the flexibility that is among the best qualities of any truly capitalist economy. So two questions arise: why did the South go to war? and, more important: how did it manage to resist for four years without having at its disposition a highly flexible and efficient capitalist economy?

The truth was, as will be seen, that the South knew not only that it had no capitalist efficiency, but that it did not even want such an existence. Compelled to fight a modern, industrial war, facing a tremendously efficient and flexible capitalist war economy, the South consciously confronted the enemy on the only terms that a backward, inefficient precapitalist system might try to fight such a war: by jumping over the capitalist era into a completely new era, a sort of state socialism.

The starting point was the decision of the South to give birth to its most mature intellectual product: an independent Confederacy. Then, it had to accept war in order to defend itself, and, in the meantime, to wage war without giving up the very principles upon which its "ideal state" had been founded. This, in turn, caused defeat: an ironclad law of modern war is that any agricultural, precapitalist community is doomed to defeat when compelled to face a highly industrialized, capitalist opponent. The so-called American Civil War ushered in that terrible product of the modern era, industrial warfare; the South was the first to experience it, and was defeated. However, what was really impressive and, I believe, will never cease to excite the highest wonder was that the South managed to meet the North on its terms—industrial warfare—without giving up the agrarian, pre-capitalist structure of the South. This may seem purely utopian. But the Confederacy itself was a kingdom of utopia, doomed to defeat since its very birth. At any rate, let us study the issue more closely.

As soon as it was created, the southern Confederacy stated its ideals very clearly. It is interesting to reread both Confederate Constitutions from this viewpoint.

There is a marked difference between the two Constitutions, generated mainly by the exigence (which manifested itself when the constituents began to write the definitive one) to follow rather closely the blueprint of the existent Constitution of the United States of 1788. For this reason, several interesting ideas embodied in the provisional charter were abandoned. Nevertheless, the basic philosophy of the seigneurial civilization was the cornerstone of both Constitutions, from the provision that tended to enfeeble the political parties' dictatorship by forbidding the reelection of the incumbent President to the provision that gave the Legislature the right to call members of the Executive to the floor of the Assembly to justify their actions; from the articles that forbade pork-barrel and log-rolling legislation, meant to forestall the rise of a class of professional politicians as in the North, to that which allowed the President to veto single parts of bills; from the prohibition against protective duties to the authorization given to single states to pursue federal officials guilty of anything against a state. This would have been indeed the "ideal state" of southern aristocratic planters.

On this, some reflections must be made. In the West Indies the seigneurial class never rose to such power, prestige, and self-consciousness as to attempt the organization of a government of its own. In Brazil, the seigneurial class lived under the delusion of being in power, as, in fact, it was. But the power the seigneurial class possessed was only enough to prevent it from grasping real power, not enough to forestall the rise—inside its own state—of new bourgeois groups, which, at last, overthrew its power from inside. However, as at least part of the planter class of the Old South survived the Civil war (only its political class, the flower of southern civilization, was destroyed), so the seigneurial class of Brazil survived the abolition of slavery to which, it must be said, it put up a fierce resistance. Only in Mexico was the *hacendado* class overthrown by a bloody struggle, the Mexican Revolution and civil war. In other parts of Spanish America the whole social structure collapsed, so that, either the seigneurial class was merged into the bourgeoisie (mainly of *compradores*) and liquidated with them (Cuba), or mixed in bloody, internecine struggle with bourgeois and popular groups, as in other parts of Latin America; or even swept aside by agrarian *reformas* (Peru).

Only in the United States was the section ruled by seigneurial planters confronted by an extremely modern, dynamic, and powerful capitalist society on the verge of entering an industrial revolution, a society that could no longer afford to have the planter civilization live autonomously inside the Union like an extraneous body.

What the Republican Party proposed to do amounted, in fact, to the drastic liquidation of planters' power by "limiting" slavery inside the states where it existed, so that, as Senator Sumner said, it could die like a pestiferous rat in its den. Sometimes words kill more than deeds. Compelling the proud, authoritarian seigneurial class to accept such second-rate citizenship inside the Union, to bow and become a kind of "corrupted member" of the social body, spotted by the sinful and loathsome stain of slavery, would have done more in the way of destroying it as a class than the platonic prohibition against expanding slavery into an area where nobody really wanted to bring it. The second step would have been to impose over the South a tariff policy that would have stopped forever any attempt to establish direct commercial links with other, more distant markets (Great Britain, France) and made southern agriculture completely subservient to northern industry. In this way the already existing colonial status of the South would have been riveted around its feet like a chain, and the South deprived, *de facto*, of any power inside the Union.

Faced by a similar issue several years later, the Brazilian planters chose the way of passive, indirect resistance; and still, for them, the immediate problem seemed to be only that of abolishing slavery, not being transformed into a completely colonial province. The fact was, as already stressed, that in Brazil, slaverholders' power was attacked from inside; in the Old South, from outside. As a matter of fact, the southern seigneurial class was aware of being the leader of an entirely separated nation.

Antonio Gramsci once said that the key to almost any great fight in the capitalist era's history is the struggle between town and country. Capitalist bourgeoisie, as its very name suggests, is a purely urban class, which tends to subdue the agrarian societies, compelling them to contribute to the primary accumulation of capital to be invested in the industrialization process. The country (taken as a whole, great landowners, farmers, yeomen) does resist, but usually, as bourgeois capitalism has greater financial and technological resources, is defeated. So it happened, when the English feudal and agrarian classes were defeated at the beginning of the modern era by the urban bourgeoisie; when the Italian bourgeoisie from the big cities of the North defeated feudal southern landowners and unified Italy—under its hegemony; and, at last, when Stalin defeated the Russian *kulaks,* compelling them by blood and iron to pay the cost of forced industrialization. However, when the critical town-country relation takes the shape of a fight between different territorial sections, the struggle becomes one of nations with diverse cultures. In the contemporary era this kind of fight —industrial countries against "backward" agrarian neighbors—is called "colonialism."

So the struggle between the North and the South fast became a question of different nationalisms—"if America was to be one nation or two," as Lincoln cogently said. The southern nation was growing slowly. No nation may rise without a self-conscious ruling class able to produce a highly sophisticated political class, founded upon a strong cultural background and tradition. As already observed, the planter civilization was something more than pure slaveholding, even if a slave economy was the social base of the so-called tropical civilization. A civilization becomes such only at the level of superstructure; it is an elusive, remarkable product of human history, very intricate and complex, something that crystallizes and becomes visible only in a superior and rarefied atmosphere. No mechanical passage can be made from economic basic structure to cultural superstructure, the stumbling block for purely "economic" historians. History, as Giambattista Vico and Benedetto Croce correctly said, is made by men and not by brute economic forces; what distinguishes men is the ability to think.

A nation of ants may produce wonderful social, and even economic, organisms; it might even be able (it is not unreasonable to suppose) to invent incredible engines. Following the fantasy of H. G. Wells, we might even imagine a community of ants wielding machines, mass producing tremendous, wonderfully organized anthills. What is absolutely impossible is to imagine a community of ants writing Shakespearian dramas, *The Divine Comedy,* Kantian *Critics,* or elaborating all those elements that compose a culture. On such ground, even the most backward Stone-Age civilization is infinite light-years ahead of an ant community. So, what was very important and striking in seigneurial civilization was the elaboration of a distinctive culture that was not born automatically of slavery nor could it have been. The basic difference between the Renaissance gentleman Sir Walter Ralegh and the Calvinist Puritan who repudiated classicism and stuck to a philosophy of hard labor and capital investment is by far more important for understanding the differences between seigneurial and capitalist civilization than the question of slavery or no slavery.

Once again, this is not to minimize the impact of slavery. What is important is to understand the relation in a dialectic way. Slavery was indispensable to the growth of southern civilization *as it was;* but it did not and could not generate *automatically* such a civilization. Seigneurial culture, indeed, was more ready than puritan society to accept slavery; conversely, slavery influenced it and later was among the most important forces to shape it.

Accordingly, the Old South had achieved what was necessary to give birth to an independent nation: a basic, individual economy, a social organization of its own, an elaborated culture, a political leading class that had reached complete self-consciousness.

At this point, what the North was asking from the South amounted simply to self-destruction. And no ruling class directing a nation on the brink of being born has ever surrendered its very existence without a fight, however desperate, preferring to die game than to surrender ignominiously.

During the last decades of its existence, the Old South had attained the highest point, one that cultures very rarely attain: the possibility of creating its "ideal state." It is perfectly true that had the South fought only to defend slavery, it could have done so better by remaining inside the Union. Brazilian slaveholders (who chose passive resistance) succeeded in defending their institution until 1888; Cuban slaveholders, until 1890. And, still, these planter classes fared better with abolition than did the southerners in the Civil War. Had the South done the same, however, it would have lost what it loved better, its own culture, its "soul." First, because it would simply have demonstrated that its culture, after all, was not worth a fight; second, because such an obscure death would have baffled the supreme aspiration of any civilization: to live in history, to hand down a proud heritage to its children.

Elsewhere, I advanced the supposition that the southern seigneurial class (through the persons of its leaders) had a complete awareness that the South was doomed and that only the opportunity of choosing the best way to die remained; [1] the more I read the papers of such men as John C. Calhoun, the more I believe this is the truth.

However, a question might arise here. Why did those men conscious of the truth, such men as Jefferson Davis and Robert E. Lee, not try to stop their fellow countrymen from plunging blindly into a war that meant defeat? Had they decided to bring the whole nation to holocaust in order to allow the South "to survive in history"? I do not want to be misunderstood. When I wrote that the most aware members of the seigneurial class felt that their civilization had only "to choose the best way to die," I meant neither that they were wickedly bringing their people down with them into some sort of *Götterdämmerung* nor that they had any clear-cut rational certainty of what was going to happen. The fact was that such consciousness (as may easily be seen from their writings, speeches, and letters) was at the level of a feeling or, better, of an ominous presage—not enough, certainly, for descending into the streets and asking people to surrender—on the basis of what? Some "presage"? Nobody would have followed them. Indeed, such spiritual processes never go beyond the threshold of rational conscience, never go farther than the area that Carl Gustav Jung calls the area of "feelings." They can be more or less clear; they certainly constitute a basic self-awareness, but they cannot become the basis for any rational, concrete political action. It is almost useless to stress that, when speaking of class-consciousness, we do not speak of any rationally demonstrable certainty but of a sphere of feelings that springs from the very depth of the collective unconscious, where lies buried the very "cultural" heritage of generations.

A closer study, I believe, would reveal that almost everybody in the Old South had more or less reached such an awareness, but in the greatest number of southerners it remained deeply concealed inside their subconscious or semi-conscious strata. The very enthusiasm for fighting, the deadly decision to go headlong into war, even the apparently foolish contempt toward the "nation of shopkeepers which would not fight," can be assumed (as any psychologist would in all likelihood agree) as singular manifestations from "sacred victims," marching to holocaust. Any supreme decision prompted by the conviction that "it is better to die game than go ahead living this way" is characteristic of people who have already decided to give up their lives, families, properties, putting them into the hands of the God of Battles, and have already discounted the perspective of death as of no relevance.

So it was that the South accepted war—and could not really have done differently.

As for the second question posed at the beginning of this chapter, it must be stressed that it is amply clear that the South, from the very beginning, was perfectly aware of courting death. This is demonstrated by the bare fact that southern leaders understood from the beginning the kind of war they had to fight. They knew the North well, with its tremendous economic and industrial might, and reacted in a correct way, as far as preparation was concerned. So, let us consider the kind of war the South had to confront, and the means it might use for confronting it.

The American seigneurial civilization, from its very birth down to 1861, ranged over a span of about three hundred and fifty years. Yet a man born when Ralegh was still alive—either in Brazil or in the West Indies or in Viriginia or even a man living in South Carolina at the beginning of the eighteenth century, a contemporary of Eliza Lucas Pinckney, who might have been resurrected in the Old South at the rise of the Confederacy —would have found himself in a wholly familiar social *milieu*. Among the most striking features of seigneurial society was its immobilism—indeed, very few societies had ever been so static. Between the South Carolina of early 1700 and that of 1861 there was almost no difference—the same hierarchic organization, the same social culture, the same backward way of cultivating the land. Had this man been from the rice district, the crops and the way slaves worked the rice fields would have been familiar to him. Incidentally, this would, by itself, destroy the pretense that the southern civilization was "capitalistic." As Marx adroitly observed, what most characterizes capitalist society is its high grade of dynamism. In the Old South, stillness was the basic aspect. So, a man born on an eighteenth-century Virginia or South Carolina plantation would have found absolutely no trouble in adapting himself to plantation life in 1861.

Instead, how different the case of a man born in a capitalistic society of the eighteenth century and transported into the same area one hundred and sixty years later! Mercantile capitalism had everywhere all but disappeared, or was about to disappear; in its place were big industrial plants powered by steam engines. Cities were booming beyond any imagination; old factories or artisan shops were no more to be found; economically, socially, technically, politically, the new industrial world would be beyond comprehension for our bewildered Rip Van Winkle.

However, what was more important was the fact that, beginning with the French Revolution, capitalism had totally abandoned the way of warfare known in the eighteenth century, introducing in exchange a tremendously new one, destined to have the most dramatic consequences to mankind.

When General Oglethorpe crossed the Savannah River to enter Georgia, war was being waged everywhere by professional standing armies. The bourgeois class, then not yet in power, except in Great Britain, was content to keep for itself the control of trade and manufacturing, leaving politics and war to absolute kings. England was no exception, since not needing an army because the royal navy protected its shores from invasions, it had not followed the example of Cromwell's "New Model." Later, the "glorious revolution" had given to the bourgeois class control even of politics; but war, being the business of a relatively narrow number of specialists, was still the right of professionals, mainly in the Admiralty. At any rate, the British kingdom was the exception confirming the rule, as land warfare was everywhere the private dominion of absolute kings and their officers, all coming from landed nobility. The European kings were by no means so foolish as to put weapons in the hands of their people; nor did they wish any kind of a total war, which might have overthrown the very social structure in which they lived and wielded power. So, warfare had to be limited, in order to make the enemy more amenable to their will without destroying him and without pushing people to revolution by means of looting or other disturbances.

For this reason armies had to be composed of professionals, serving for long terms on a mercenary basis and kept together by an iron discipline. Such soldiers usually fought well; as professionals, they were good, fighting with neither love nor hate, but only for the sake of money. They usually did their business in a skilled way, even without putting their souls into it.

Such a tool was obviously a very costly one. Soldiers had to be paid well (or they would have deserted to a better paying boss, much like the professional baseball players of today); they had to receive their pay regularly, or they would have fought badly or not at all; they had even to be well fed and well clothed, furnished with tents and camping implements, and, obviously, with good weapons and plenty of ammunition. All this had to be done without in any way disturbing the civilians. Consequently, the army required large magazines and wagon trains, supplied by local purchase on the basis of cash payment. This kind of army was expensive and, therefore, it had to be limited in size, because in that era of still relatively small-scale banking, it was not always easy to secure the money to meet the multifarious expenses it entailed. To this, it must be added that uniforms, implements, and weapons came from factories of a preindustrial era, which were capable of yielding only a small production daily.

These reasons contrived to keep armies on a relatively small scale, and moved kings to use them very carefully, as it was not easy to make good losses of men and matériel. Obviously, engagements were as few as possible, the best way to win being to compel the enemy to accept one's local and general superiority without giving battle. Although pitched and bloody battles were fought, nobody ever dreamed of driving an enemy to his knees or of winning anything like a "total" victory in the strategic field. Anybody entertaining such ideas would have been deemed crazy and more fit for the lunatic asylum than for commanding in the field. As far as the Old South was concerned, it would have found this kind of warfare wholly congenial and obvious in 1861 as in 1700; however, in the world at large, dramatic changes had occurred, making anything like this utterly impossible in the nineteenth century.

First, there had been the French Revolution. It had swept away absolute monarchy, nobility, and clergy; it had put all powers in the hands of the bourgeois class. It had given a tremendous boost to the industrial revolution even in France, opening the market to the forces that generated it. When the First Coalition arose to bring down revolutionary power, any kind of limited warfare was no longer possible. Now, war was no longer waged "inside" the system but outside; now two completely different social organizations confronted each other, both trying, not only to defeat, but even to sweep the other one off the face of the earth. So, at least to the revolutionary ruling class, war had to be total in its objectives. In the minds of French revolutionaries, this war was to be waged no longer by kings who considered the state their property, but by the "nation," whose limits were uncertain and were to be identified by vague signs of tradition, language, etc. So they were establishing the basis for the contemporary idea of a nation-state, supposed to be always right (one is tempted to say, "mainly when it happens to be wrong"), which must be founded upon a national market, dominated by capitalism, and integrated into the world market. The nation not being—as kings had been—a defender of "private" interests, everybody had to transform himself into a soldier to defend it. But, as citizens were supposed to fight because of a "sacred" duty, they did not need to be paid, so that, in the words of an officer, calling a man to arms became far less expensive than buying a mule. Additionally, as there were plenty of citizens (contrary to the situation with mules), generals might now spend more freely of the ample sum of blood at their disposition than had been the case with the limited warfare of professional armies, when casualties had been difficult to replace.

Going to war is a hard, dirty business. Contradicting rhetoric, men are usually peaceful. It is a very difficult task to take a citizen from his family, his home, his peaceful job and send him to starve, to kill, to risk death, to risk wounds, mutilations, sufferings beyond imagination, to sleep on the bare ground, to live miserably through mud, filth, blood, without persuading him that he is making such inhumane sacrifices for something "worthwhile." When France was invaded by the Coalition, this persuasion was rather easily achieved, since the Revolutionary Army was composed mainly of the bourgeoisie and yeomen who both had received great benefits from the new regime. But, as such ideal conditions rarely occur, it would soon become necessary to "persuade" men by means of a new tool: war propaganda. When war aims in themselves happen to be very far from noble and right, no matter; propaganda can persuade people that they are so. Obviously, the first propaganda tool is to persuade the populace that the enemy is ferocious, bestial, intending to destroy, so that the war is always one "for life and children." This introduced into warfare the tremendous weapon of hate, in turn moving "us" to act against the enemy as cruelly and pitilessly as he is supposed to be willing to deal with us. And, consequently, is not the best way to settle the question definitely that of utterly destroying the enemy, trampling him under our feet, so that the "danger" will be forever averted? [2]

But, as Hegel said, there is no lie that does not include at least a grain of truth. So, leaving aside propaganda, in the wars of the French Revolution the limited aims of the absolutist era were no more possible. Two different social systems were facing each other, and neither of them wanted to compromise. The very aim of both was to eliminate the other, as far as possible, so as to create a new "equilibrium" or to reinstate the old. Propaganda was a powerful tool for such an aim. So, total war, wholly unknown to the eighteenth century, made its sinister appearance in the world.

The idea was, in itself, nothing new. Italy had been called (and was) the very cradle of the bourgeois class. It is no wonder, therefore, to see national conscription first suggested there by Machiavelli.[3] During the French Revolution, this idea returned as the basis for the new national army. At the Convention, as Barère clearly stressed: ". . . *Le contingent de la France pour sa liberté comprend toute sa population, toute son industrie, tous ses travaux, tout son génie. . . .*" [4]

The bourgeois class, by sweeping away the old regime with its inefficient administrative order, its fetters, its chronic slowness, had showed the amazed world what tremendous strength lay buried inside a nation. By means of its new, centralized administration it had realized the almost incredible task of universal conscription; by means of war propaganda it had made its tremendous masses ready to fight and to die, uncompromising, full of hate toward the enemy. As Robespierre said in clear-cut terms, "the Republic had to give to enemies of liberty only death."

Of course, this involved—and made possible—logistics that were totally new. Dreaming of magazines, supply columns, and wagon trains laden with victuals and clothes for such an immense army was, for the time being, all but impossible. However, the exceptional eruption of the will to fight, created by revolutionary propaganda, made it possible for French generals to take care of all of this. Their army possessed something that no monarchical army ever possessed: an inconquerable faith in its cause. So, it was no longer necessary to keep closed lines, lest mercenaries would desert; citizen-soldiers never deserted, and might, because of this, be split into divisions and corps, able to march separately and then rejoin on the battlefield. The absence of supply columns and magazines gave such an army an impressive mobility. As for its living, it had to live off enemy country. After all, this sort of pillage was only a part of the punishment the enemy "rightly deserved."

Napoleon, by means of his genius, totally grasped the potentialities inherent in such an army and brought it to amazing victories, at least until, as he himself observed, his foe "learnt the business." He was the man who built the new, bourgeois, and capitalist France into a unified and centralized nation-state, so achieving what the Republic had just begun. But what is most important for the purpose of this book, he was the first to understand the new mass strategy made possible by conscription and national armies. This could be seen mainly in the Russian campaign. Contrary to what is usually assumed, Napoleon's Russian campaign was planned in a very sound way; it ranks among the best-planned campaigns of the Emperor. Even the so-called disastrous retreat was handled skillfully, so that losses were limited to a minimum, considering the circumstances. What created the appalling episode of the Berezina, so well dramatized by Tolstoi, were mainly bands of stragglers; the bulk of the army never allowed the retreat to become a rout.

Of immense interest is the fact that Napoleon had made use, for the first time in this campaign, of the immense armies that conscription and the new organics and logistics had made possible. He advanced for the first time in history with a whole army group over an immense front and showed how it was possible to handle such tremendous strength. No absolute king had ever dared dream of anything like it. One has only to compare the invasion of Russia by Charles XII of Sweden to the Napoleonic thrust to be amazed.

Nevertheless, the invasion was a failure. Why? Napoleon had foreseen with accuracy the nature of future warfare in the new bourgeois-capitalist world. He failed because he was too far ahead of his time. What he built was a tremendous body—with no bones. Because of the scorched-earth strategy adopted by the Russians (and because the revolutionary enthusiasm had in large part melted away), it was necessary to supply the great army adequately. This could not be done over muddy roads with slow-moving wagon trains and pack mules. The means of communication were also lacking. The enormous, boneless body collapsed under its sheer weight.

In other words, the French Revolution had created mass armies but had been unable to create mass warfare. The necessary implements to allow such a qualitative stride were almost ready at hand, however. The industrial revolution had already won in Great Britain; it was going ahead by gigantic steps in France. If we look at it, it is easy to see that no revolution in history, except perhaps the neolithic one, had ever been so . . . revolutionary. Until then, the center of human productivity had been the country. Industries, as discussed earlier, had been wholly subordinated to agriculture, their task being mainly to complete the process of agrarian production. It is interesting to observe that in old-fashioned societies, mines were considered as belonging to agriculture; in fact, men used to say that they were "cultivated," like fields. Indeed, when the industrial revolution exploded, with its voracious appetite for coal, iron, copper, lead, and other minerals, old mines were for the most part abandoned as small, superficial and worthless, except in such old-fashioned, agrarian countries as the Old South. Now the center of production was transferred to cities. Engines became all-powerful, in any sense. As it was correctly said, mankind was throwing God down from altars and putting a machine in His place.

Obviously, the industrial revolution did not come out of nothing. Its deep roots are to be found in northern Italy, where, in the eleventh and twelfth centuries the new bourgeois class was born in city-states. "To understand the basic meaning of the rise of such urban centers," wrote Carlo Cipolla, "it is necessary to stress their revolutionary aspect, the harsh and violent revolt against the dominating agrarian feudal society. At that time began the end of a society whose political power and economic resources were based mainly on land property, and were monopolized by classes whose ideals were war, hunting, and praying. Instead of them, a new class began to rise, a class founded upon trade and manufacture, looking as ideals to matters of fact and money." [5]

From that time onward, the bourgeoisie—and capitalism—went on, growing and growing, and more and more tending toward a kind of mechanized production. A decisive step was made at the very threshold of the modern age, when such men as Leonardo, Michelangelo, Sir Francis Bacon, and—above any others—Galileo and Newton created the scientific and philosophic basis for the future machine age. In that era, mercantile capitalism took the place of the old bourgeois city-state. But, like Napoleon in the Russian campaign, the modern bourgeoisie still lacked the bones to build a new, gigantic world in its own image.

In a few years, however, James Watt invented an efficient steam engine. Machine tools soon followed, giving birth to the gigantic textile industry of England. In a few generations, the production of iron, coal, and textiles skyrocketed, sweeping away totally old-fashioned artisan shops and factories and transforming hundreds of thousands of men into an industrial army of wage earners (followed by a second, essential multitude: the "industrial reserve army" of unemployed). The world market was upset by tremendous crises, which, in most cases, changed it radically: I have already discussed the transformation of the Old South into the "cotton kingdom," prompted by the pressure of the international capitalist world market. Colonial and semicolonial countries now had to adjust to the new needs of industrial capitalism. What must be observed here is that the Old South was being attracted by this "cotton revolution" into the British semicolonial area, which was certainly not welcome to northern capitalists. But more about this later.

The industrial revolution swept Great Britain, creating mass production and what Marx appropriately termed "an appalling amount of commodities." Soon, colonial countries were required to absorb a large part of such commodities, sending to the mother countries their raw products. The French Revolution, in turn, demolished any obstacle to the definitive triumph of the industrial revolution, and France soon entered the race. The northern United States began its industrial revolution more or less with the War of 1812. In 1820 the new northern industrial bourgeoisie launched its first attack against the South. It failed, however, to land its blows. The industrial capitalism of the East Coast had to await the rise of agrarian capitalism in the Middle West, thus splitting the so-called agrarian front and isolating the South. For this, a major development of railroads was required.

In 1813 Robert Fulton had made what amounted to, at that time, the biggest American contribution to the industrial revolution: the steam-propelled ship. Soon Morse was to follow with a far more revolutionary device: the electric telegraph. In the beginning, quick-minded southerners had welcomed such tools, persuaded perhaps that the new industrial devices might nourish their small-scale industry and at the same time remain subordinated to agriculture. Perhaps the new steamers would help export cotton, after all. However, even if the first steamer to cross the Atlantic had sailed from Savannah, Georgia, southern planters soon had to realize how mistaken they had been. Certainly cotton was being more and more exported by steamships, that was true, but they were sailing from New York and under northern flags. As a matter of fact, the new mechanical tools were better handled by industrial states, which had the necessary capital to produce them *en masse* and the skilled labor, concentrated in large factories and shipyards, to build them.

Napoleon died in 1821, when the industrial revolution had

already set the preliminary conditions for a revolution in warfare. England had become "the workshop of the world," which Napoleon had much feared. Now the engine was ready to join the sword, or, better, to relegate it to a secondary place.

Deadly inventions followed one another with an astonishing speed. In 1784 Henry Shrapnel invented his shell case; very soon, advanced metallurgy created cannon able to fire them by the score. This branch of industry progressed so quickly that in a few years it became possible to realize the dream of firing large explosive shells (heretofore used only by mortars) horizontally by means of cannon. The French Directory had created a special commission to study such a possibility, but it was not until 1822 that General Henri Paixhans built an effective gun that was able to fire large mortar shells of 8 inches with deadly precision. Until then, such shells had been used only for siege warfare. The consequences of Paixhans's invention were appalling. At the Battle of Trafalgar in 1805, not a single vessel had been sunk by artillery fire—the big, three-decker ships of the line had reached such perfection as to be virtually unsinkable. Now, during the testing of his new gun, Paixhans demonstrated how a large war vessel could be sunk by just three shells. The era of wooden ships was at an end. However, the new ironworks created by the machine age were more than able to roll tremendous iron plates, so that, in the Crimean War, both Great Britain and France built steam-propelled ironclads; the gigantic struggle between gun and armor had begun.

Even infantry weapons were revolutionized. In 1800, thanks to the progress of chemistry, fulminate of mercury was invented, making possible the adoption of copper percussion caps, invented in their turn in 1816, and the consequent elimination of now obsolete flintlocks, which could not fire in the rain. In 1849 Claude Étienne Minié invented the cylindro-conical bullet, which expanded under the pressure of gas, thus fitting into the rifling. The first effective rifled gun was able to kill a man at a distance of 1200 to 1300 yards, whereas the old smoothbore musket had been all but ineffective at more than a hundred yards. This weapon, in the hands of the soldiers of a mass army, was able to create a deadly shower of bullets

previously undreamed of. In 1845 General Cavalli, of the Sardinian Army, invented a rifled, breech-loading cannon, with a range and accuracy up to that time wholly unknown.

These deadly weapons were, in themselves, enough to wholly revolutionize old-style warfare. But what achieved a truly complete revolution—and furnished the iron "bones" that Napoleon had lacked in the Russian campaign—were three products of the industrial revolution that originally had absolutely nothing to do with war. First, the railroad. The first effective railroad had been inaugurated in 1825, the engine having been invented by George Stephenson. In a few years, Great Britain, France, the United States, and even Prussia were covered by wide railroad networks. In this way, the railway train, together with the steamship, had completely solved the gigantic problem of transporting enormous amounts of troops and supplies; logistics would never be the same. Friedrich List pointed out correctly that a good railroad network offered "speed of mobilization, the rapidity with which troops could be moved from the centre of the country to its periphery, and the other obvious advantages of 'interior lines.' " [6]

The second invention to transform warfare was the electric telegraph, which all but solved the problem of handling enormous masses of soldiers on different and far distant fronts. The third and most important invention was the means of production: mass production, which was wholly unknown to an earlier age. Railroads and mass armies and the telegraph wire could not do the job alone. It was necessary to turn out at an amazing speed tons of ammunition, thousands of ordnance pieces, millions of bullets and shells, hundreds of locomotives, railroad cars, steamships, iron plates, thousands of tons of explosives, thousands of yards of cloth, hundreds of thousands of pairs of shoes.

Through these developments, mass armies had found, at last, their "iron bones." However, these bones were fast becoming the monopoly of industrial countries, able to field another, and even larger, army, composed of thousands of engineers, hundreds of thousands of skilled workers, mechanics, smelters, plumbers, even electricians; all backed by enormous industrial apparatuses, thousands of miles of railroads, thousands of ships, hundreds of shipyards, hundreds of repair shops; and all this, in turn, able to produce at such speed and in such quantity as to overwhelm the enemy. The tremendous era of industrial warfare loomed large on the horizon; as General John Fuller wrote, the ironmonger was ready to displace the general.

Baron Henri Jomini did correctly foresee that war was soon to take on apocalyptic dimensions, to become "a most unreasonable struggle" aimed at destroying the enemy, the return of barbarous ages, so that mankind might be forced to live once again through the eras of Vandals, Huns, and Tartars.

This was the kind of war that the Old South faced, while throughout this mighty industrial revolution, the South itself had not changed at all. Some industrial devices, the railroads, the telegraph, entered the South, to be sure, but it remained an agrarian area, absolutely deprived of anything like mass industry or mass production. The North, on the other hand, had totally changed. Unlike the cavalier of the eighteenth century who would have felt at home in the South of 1861, a Yankee of the puritan age would have been lost in the incredible, maddening industrial New England of the mid-nineteenth century. In fact, the North had developed into an industrial giant.

Having answered the first question, Why did the South accept war? and the second, What kind of war did the Old South have to face? we are now confronted with a third question: How could the agrarian South engage in the new technological warfare, engage a superior enemy supported by the weapons of industry?

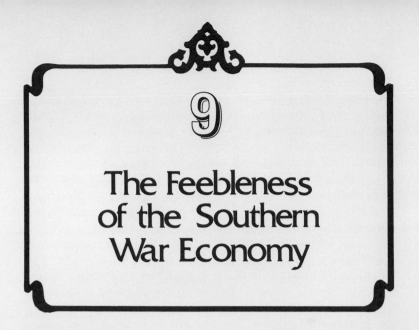

The Feebleness of the Southern War Economy

When the French invaded Algeria in 1830, the old-fashioned army of the bey was disposed of very easily. But before the invaders could be proclaimed victorious, a new, terrible kind of warfare erupted. Led mainly by men from the old feudal class (the most prominent being Abd-el-Kader), the Algerians staged a tremendous guerrilla attack that soon put the invaders in an extremely awkward situation. It required almost twenty years of massacre and wholesale killing to end the business, and although Abd-el-Kader was compelled to surrender, guerrilla warfare never really stopped, continuing off and on for more than a century, until Algeria won its independence.

Algeria is perhaps one of the most striking examples of guerrilla warfare. But there are more. In 1861 Italy was unified. In the Kingdom of the Two Sicilies, the old Bourbonist army was defeated by Garibaldi in a lightning campaign, which culminated in the major battle of the Volturno. What remained of that army, together with the king and the royal family, was besieged by the Italian army in the fortresses of Capua, Gaeta, and Civitella del Tronto. Southern Italy seemed all but subdued. The victors felt confident, and immediately "forgot" what Garibaldi, more democratically, had pledged to the poor peasantry of the south: to distribute the great lands of the public domain. Worst of all, the old feudal landowners, certainly despotic and oppressive, but also, in many cases (like the old "Leopard," so well depicted by Tomasi di Lampedusa), good-natured and paternalist, were replaced by bourgeois landowners. They had bought large properties at low prices and now were beginning to exact hard and "productive" work. Moreover, some "benefits" of a modern, capitalist state were introduced abruptly, among them taxes and conscription.

The poorest part of the peasantry found themselves with their backs to the wall and were more than ready to take to the mountains. Consequently, armed bands were formed and immediately styled "brigands" by the Italian administration. After a few halfhearted attempts to quell the insurrection by some too-little and too-late reforms, the government gave all power to General Enrico Cialdini, quite sure that the modern Italian army could easily crush such illiterate "savages." However, it was not so; and a true civil war, which created victims by the thousands, raged for almost ten years throughout southern Italy. In the end, the army found itself almost powerless and had to resort to police-like operations.

So, in both these situations, an invaded people (in each case agrarian and "backward") had resorted to the only strategy useful in defying a modern mass army and its deadly weapons: guerrilla warfare. Assuredly, the example was not new. The first insurrection of contemporary times had been that of the yeomen of the Vendée against the French Republican Army; and the French generals spent several years in crushing it. Then Spain resorted to guerrilla fighting against Napoleon's army; the same happened in Russia, where the name "partisan" had its birth.

This possible means for a colonial, agrarian people to resist against modern armies had not escaped the attention of theorists. In 1823, in Paris, Jean Frédéric Auguste Le mière de Corvey published his book *Des partisans et des Corps irrégulieres* which may be considered the first organic treatise on guerrilla warfare; it was followed in 1830 by what was to be the definitive textbook on the subject: *Della Guerra d'Insurre-*

sione per Bande, written in Paris by a distinguished Sardinian officer during his exile there because of his liberal ideas. Count Carlo Bianco di Saint-Jorioz even published, three years later, a practical manual for guerrilla warfare.[1] Bianco's works had a not indifferent follower in America: no less than John Brown.[2] At any rate, partisan warfare clearly stood out as the only technique an agrarian community could use against a powerful industrial nation; it would eventually become the chosen way of waging war for any colonial people in the nineteenth and twentieth centuries.

So the question is: had the South any idea of resorting to this kind of warfare? The answer can be given quickly and categorically: absolutely not, even if, later, during the war, southern partisans would have gladly played a part. From the very beginning, as the first acts of Confederate authorities clearly show, the South was girding for a great industrial war, face to face with the invaders. In other words, the South was accepting the kind of war most congenial to its foe. In a war like this, it had almost every probability of being defeated. Why did the South accept *this* kind of war?

A satisfying answer has yet to be found. One might venture to surmise that since the South, inside its innermost soul, was deadly sure of being doomed, it chose the most spectacular way of dying, that which allowed it to live in history. Historical life does not usually come to people who resort to guerrilla warfare, their destiny being that future historians almost ignore or at least underrate them. Everybody knows the events of the American Civil War; but the battles of the Vendée or of the Spanish insurgents or of southern Italian peasants are only vaguely known, if at all.[3] This explanation is, of course, impossible to demonstrate by ordinary historic tools. But let me add some additional qualifications.

When the American Civil War exploded, the southern slave society was on the very brink of crumbling. Not because of immediate economic motives (slavery might still be "profitable," and slaveholders might even be "sanguine"; although after a careful reading of their private letters, certainly not intended for other people and full of concern about abolitionist campaigns, etc., one would not easily dare to warrant it), but because of the moral issue. Waging partisan warfare against a northern Army firmly established in the midst of southern territory and at the same time keeping slaves faithful to their masters was almost impossible.

Algeria was able to maintain its slave society, because its slavery was still almost purely domestic and the slave society was very far from the critical point already reached in the South. The same can be said of the Brazilian war against the Dutch in the mid-seventeenth century. Southerners succeeded in waging effective partisan warfare on a limited scale (Mosby being the most striking example), but a mass partisan warfare in a country of slaves who very soon would become disaffected would have been a risky gamble indeed. At any rate, it would have meant the almost immediate collapse of the seigneurial world. Without its "space," it would have been doomed. Consequently the only move left to slaveholders was to accept the "rules" laid down by the enemy: a big industrial war.

On this battlefield, the South had one major asset: like any agrarian community, it was particularly rich in what Antonio Gramsci called "traditional intellectuals"—lawyers, philosophers, scientists, scholars, practitioners of "pure" science. While the North, like any technological society, had a majority of "organics," or urban intellectuals—engineers, managers, technicians. Gramsci underlined that the "creative" function is most often performed by "traditional intellectuals," a true "intelligentsia," while "organic intellectuals" are stronger in the executive, managerial fields.[4]

It might be said that the North had undoubtedly the more pragmatic spirit, more practical, shrewd, businesslike, matter-of-fact men; the South had more inventive minds, more given to fantasy, a higher degree of genius. Summing up, the South lacked those elements required by modern warfare, with two exceptions: a will to fight (little propaganda was needed to mobilize a mass army and being a country people, a potentially excellent infantry and cavalry were at hand) and a high quality creative leadership generated from its "traditional intellectuals." What the South totally lacked was an industrial orga-

nization directed and managed by an expert capitalist class. To create such an organization, from almost nothing and without the social structure of an industrial society, was a formidable task.

To understand this point, consideration must be given to the condition of southern factories and commercial facilities as the South undertook to fight the first large industrial war, the greatest to be fought anywhere on earth, excepting the two world wars.

Both the industrial and commercial situations in the South were, from this standpoint, all but a disaster. As frequently stressed, the South *did* have industry; that was not the problem. The correct question to ask is what *kind* of industry? Eugene D. Genovese has pointed out the factors that hampered any serious industrial development in the slave states: "another factor," he writes, "which in itself provides an adequate explanation of the South's inability to industrialize, [was] the retardation of the home market for both industrial and agricultural commodities. . . . Industrialization is unthinkable without an agrarian revolution which shatters the old regime on the countryside." [5] The South had no relevant market to justify an industry: "The opinion of the editor of the *Southern Agriculturalist* in 1828, that the South lacked sufficient customers to sustain a high level of manufacturing, echoed throughout the ante-bellum period." [6] In this area, a fact of utmost importance has been frequently overlooked: the only sizable iron factory of the Old South, the famous Tredegar Iron Works of Richmond, Virginia, managed to survive by limiting practically all its production to ordnance and ordnance stores, sold to the U.S. government.[7] This, to economists, is a well-known characteristic of backward countries and denotes a pathological, not a healthy, industrialization. Let me refer again to the example of Italy.

After its unification, Italy, like the Old South, had an exceedingly poor internal market. Per capita income in Italian lire was 196 yearly, as against 200 for the Austrian Empire, 428 for Prussia, 650 for France, and 775 for Great Britain.[8] Consequently, consumption of goods was very low and the market was poor, so that when the Italian ruling class entered a major program of industrialization, the biggest plants to rise in Italy were great ironworks, whose production (heavy guns and iron plates for warships) had to be almost completely sold to a single customer: the Italian government. Very cogently, the poet of Italian imperialism, Gabriele D'Annunzio, was singing, in the last of his ten "Canzoni d'Oltremare":

Ah! My Country! You didn't need ten songs:
Ten Ironclads,
Hammered by the same strong love over the anvil;
And not connected syllables:
Iron plates, welded together by burning hammers . . .[9]

The South, pursuing no imperialistic policy, but only trying to survive, did not need a D'Annunzio to persuade its public that its own major ironworks had to produce exclusively for the government. Before the war, planters had not concerned themselves with Tredegar. Actually, they were hostile to industrialization, and with good cause, for they needed only as much industry as was required to supply some of their needs—coarse clothing for slaves, some agricultural tools—in any case, not more of an industry than might be kept under the stringent control of agriculture. A large iron factory like Tredegar could survive in the Old South only on government orders.[10] Such advocates of early industrialization as J. D. B. DeBow were left preaching in the desert; planters fostered only such industries as were of immediate interest to them, and in many cases such factories were owned by the planters themselves.[11]

To further illustrate the desperate industrial inferiority of the Old South, a consideration of the progress in metallurgy is required. Since 1850, with the introduction of anthracite-iron, metallurgy had made a tremendous qualitative jump from old-fashioned to modern technology. In the North the giant ironworks of Pittsburgh, Pennsylvania, New York, and New England were adopting the new techniques, sustained by large capital investments and a tremendous development of coal mining, while in the South, this kind of production was still in its infancy. Southern ironworks still relied almost completely on charcoal iron, produced by small agricultural furnaces scattered across the countryside, wherever there was plenty of wood, as in the almost forgotten times of the early Iron Age. Of course, charcoal iron was, at that time, better than anthracite iron, more tensile, freer from sulfur, but it cost twice as much.[12] The development of a modern iron industry required a philosophy that was, to the South, all but untenable: the conception of converting from the old agricultural age of small, scattered, almost artisan furnaces to tremendous, concentrated units of mining and casting, requiring enormous amounts of capital investment, a whole generation of industrial managers, engineers, technicians, skilled workmen—the advent of an urban, capitalist civilization rather than a backward agricultural society.

In the contemporary era, the Chinese government encouraged the rise of small, scattered blast furnaces, owned and managed by local agrarian communities. A comparison between what happened in the Old South a hundred years ago and in China today might be very interesting, as, in both cases, an agrarian iron industry, based on local workshops, had the aim of preventing the rise of a large, industrial and technological class; bourgeois-managerial capitalism in the first instance, Soviet-style bureaucratic technocracy in the second. However, in the case of the South, such resistance was not planned; it was created by objective situations, a lack of capital, the absence of modern urban life, a lack of managers and a large army of skilled workmen and wage earners, complemented by the inevitable labor-reserve army of the unemployed.

This then was the situation before the Civil War. Later, what had been only a *de facto* situation became planned, in a way oddly similar to what Chinese leaders did in a totally different context. Another strange consequence was that, thanks to Tredegar's almost exclusive military production, the Confederacy, at the very moment of its direst need, had at hand a good cannon foundry and rolling mill.

However, it must be remembered that Tredegar, as the only factory able to cast heavy ordnance throughout the South before the war, made the position of the city of Richmond terribly important and a true nightmare for southern generals. Still, no rolling mill, not even Tredegar, could produce two-inch plates. The total production of iron in the southern states amounted to only 12 percent of that of the North. The South had thirty-nine furnaces producing 26,262 tons of pig iron, whereas northern production went well over 160,000 tons.[13]

As far as coal was concerned, production began in Virginia and Alabama on a very limited scale. The Confederacy had other coal supplies in North Carolina and Georgia, lead in Virginia and east Tennessee, and deposits of many other ores in various locations, with the exception of mercury. However, generally, the ore was extracted only from small mines or not at all.[14] In the important field of explosives, the "industrial" production of the southern states was almost farcical. In all, they possessed only two artisan workshops, one in Tennessee, with ten workers, and another in South Carolina, with three.[15] Summing up, the production of crude and bar iron, coal, garments, cotton sheeting, woolens, and shoes in the seceded states was not more than 8 to 14 percent of that of the northern states.[16]

While the industrial situation was almost catastrophic, the agricultural prospects might have far surpassed those of the North, as the Confederacy produced "nearly all of the rice, sugar, sweet potatoes, peas and beans in the United States, and a substantial wheat crop. Draft and food animals were abundant, although inferior in quality. Cotton land could be converted to augment food production and still leave sufficient cotton for producing textiles and as barter for purchasing supplies." [17] These facts were certainly true; however, inadequate transportation created serious problems for the distribution of such foodstuffs throughout the Confederacy—and to the Confederate army. This was the situation, then, enough indeed to chill Confederate bones, if only the leaders had not had such deadly dedication.

To enter the war with a minimum probability of survival, the Confederacy, obviously, had to industrialize—or die. Compounding the lack of industry were inadequate transportation systems and an almost nonexistent commercial network. These problems were, of course, linked—the vicious circle. No industrialization is possible without a commercial organization and adequate land and water transportation systems; without industry, transportation and trade would collapse.

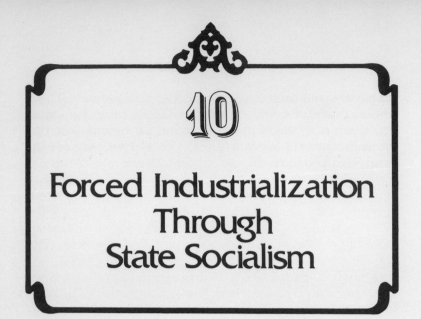

10

Forced Industrialization Through State Socialism

To industrialize an agrarian country means nothing less than introducing and achieving therein an industrial revolution that elsewhere had been accomplished in a matter of years, decades, if not centuries—and to do it walking across history with "seven-league boots."

In Great Britain, France, and the northern United States, industrialization had been achieved as the most important effect of the rise of capitalism; in turn, it had deeply affected the bourgeois class, causing the eclipse of mercantile capitalism and opening the way to industrial hegemony. Industrialization requires enormous capital investment; such capital had been accumulated slowly, through the process of "primitive accumulation," mainly at the expense of agrarian classes, so that, when the development of great industry began in earnest, enough accumulated capital was available for investment, along with an army of wage laborers to work.

This was the "physiological" process; and in Great Britain, France, and the northern United States, it had been and was being achieved under the firm hegemony of a capitalist bourgeoisie, already risen to be the ruling class of the land. In turn, the development of industrial capitalism had strengthened the bourgeoisie and completed the utter defeat of the agrarian classes, reducing them to the role of "allied" members of a new "historic bloc." This relationship was to be seen afterward in Germany, where capitalism shared power with the old-fashioned agrarian *Junker* class, relinquishing military power to the latter, together with a part of the political power, even if about 78 percent of the members of the Reichstag came from the bourgeoisie and the "new" nobility.[1] Even in Great Britain the landowning nobility had been fully rallied and was collaborating with the bourgeoisie in the army, navy, and diplomacy. The same happened later in Japan.

Assuredly, the Confederate government could not hope to set in motion such a process. First, because it had to be, more or less, "natural"; and this was certainly not the case in the Confederacy. Second, because a "natural" process (even encouraged as it was in many cases by special privileges, laws, monopolies, etc.) required time, and the Confederacy had no time to spare. Third, and most important, because such a process would have conjured up a rampaging capitalist class in the South, the ogre the Confederacy was fighting to banish. It would have been better to surrender to northern capitalism without a fight.

Consequently, the only recourse for the planter class was to resort to forced industrialization. History furnished no examples (at least, on the scale required); indeed, it was necessary to wait three more generations to see the example of Soviet Russia, which would offer a solution as breathtaking and momentous as the Confederate experiment. This sector of Confederate history is, indeed, far from being well understood. To attempt an understanding, let us consider for a moment what happened in Soviet Russia after 1925.

The problem of industrialization had been seen by the Bolsheviks well before Lenin's death, albeit, for the time being, without the urgent pressure of a danger from abroad. Bolshevik rulers knew all too well that their country had to be forever on guard, it was true, but there was no threat of immediate aggression. Consequently, they had time, at least within a reasonable scope of years. The main objective to be pursued, however, was economic independence, together with raising the standard of living of Russian workers through a larger selection of commodities. Accordingly, the Conference of the Communist Party, held in December 1925, was unanimous in favor of industrialization. But where to find capital to invest? Economically speaking, the problem of capital investment was twofold: resources to be invested and time required to achieve a satisfying standard of production.[2] Leon Trotsky, as usual the more clear-minded among Bolshevik leaders, argued that Russia would have to go through an accelerated process of primary accumulation (which he called "socialist primary accumulation" in order to stress that it would be planned). This meant that the future development of Soviet industry would depend on the amount of capital in the government's hands. The government had only two sources to tap: foreign loans and the future industrial output.

Foreign loans were not easy to get, and far too expensive for the U.S.S.R. Although it was not possible to dispense with loans altogether, they would have to be only a secondary source. On the other hand, the capital resulting from productivity would be available only *after* the building of industries. Faced with this impasse, the Soviets sought a third source: the incomes of the great mass of small farmers and yeomen. They might supply a tremendous amount of capital, simply by compelling them to yield a quantity of agricultural products far superior to the amount of industrial goods given them in exchange. This had always been the way, throughout the world, to compel the country to pay for the industrialization of towns. One must wonder, however, why the Bolsheviks, who did know history, chose to ignore the violence and bloodshed that had been necessary to convince agrarian communities to finance industrialization. As a matter of fact, they knew it all too well, since Preobrazensky even spoke of the "provisional" creation of a "colonial" relation between town and country in Soviet Russia.[3] However, the majority of the Bolshevik Central Committee, led by Stalin, was not yet ready to accept such viewpoints, since at that time the basic aim of Stalin was to overthrow Trotsky and his followers. Trotsky, as usual, had certainly had sharp foresight; but it was not yet time.

After Trotsky's downfall, Stalin made an abrupt turn. Now the task he was setting for the party was to strike down the so-called *kulaks*, or wealthy yeomen, accused of being "capitalists" (which, at least in perspective, was true). At the beginning of 1930 Stalin dramatically announced the decision "to liquidate the *kulaks* as a class" and unleashed a bloody civil war. *Kulak* property was expropriated, they were shot by the scores, deported by the thousands (ten million small farmers and yeomen were so "liquidated," by admission of Stalin himself).[4] In the meantime, forced industrialization was making tremendous strides. During the struggle against the *kulaks*, Soviet authorities had never forgotten their aim: it is calculated that 700 million pounds of wheat were "confiscated" from the *kulaks* to be used for financing forced industrialization. In the meantime, the compulsory organization of *kolkoses* put agrarian resources under the total control of the government. It is almost impossible to calculate how much the country was compelled to relinquish in order to finance the process; the economist Prokopovic has estimated that, during the czar's regime, in 1913, 10 percent of gross national income had been reserved for investment, while in 1932 the amount ranged between 24.2 and 26 percent.[5]

The darkening of the international horizon soon convinced Soviet leaders to push the process of industrialization more and more. Now it was necessary to give absolute priority to heavy industry, reducing in this way the amount of consumer goods. Stalin made it very clear: "Frequently I am questioned if it be possible to slow down a little bit. . . . No, comrades, this cannot be done. To slow down means to be late, and latecomers are defeated! The history of old Russia shows, among other things, that she was always beaten, because she was backward. . . . Our backwardness, in comparison with economically advanced countries, amounts from fifty to one hundred years. We must cover such distance in ten years. Either we succeed, or we will be crushed." [6]

War and invasion, as a matter of fact, were coming nearer and nearer. In 1933 Hitler seized power in Germany. Without its tremendous, superhuman—even inhuman—effort, the

U.S.S.R. would never have been able to resist the appalling German invasion and ultimately to defeat the Third Reich. The help given by Western powers, mainly the United States, was certainly of the utmost importance; however, it would be a major mistake to forget that the thousands of tanks, big guns, vehicles of many descriptions, the millions of machine guns, rifles, projectiles, which showered the Germans as a deadly storm, came from the big, new industrial plants created after 1929.

So, forced industrialization in the U.S.S.R. was, in the main, an amazing success: Stalin had "swept away barbarity by barbarous means"; had ushered his mighty country straight through the machine age into the nuclear age. The cost had been appalling: forced industrialization was almost totally paid for by farmers and yeomen, who were driven out of existence. But the crucial question lies elsewhere. How had it been possible to crush ten million yeomen, to manage the awesome five-year plans, to direct with iron hands such a mighty revolution? In other words: by what means had the party leaders accomplished this revolution?

Any political class, it is clear, in order to exercise its power physically has to rely on an "apparatus," a sort of secular brass that permits the transformation of the will of the political class into concrete power—the passage from planning into execution. Such an apparatus arose in the U.S.S.R. gradually. Already powerful when Trotsky was defeated and Stalin took over leadership, it continued to grow and grow afterward. The apparatus was composed of the political and technological bureaucracies, and between both groups there was an osmosis. Stalin did not want to see the technocrats grow too strong in relation to party bureaucrats, so, very soon, he gave his faithful *apparatciks* the catchword: "It is indispensable to master technology." [7] By means of an always present, protean bureaucracy, Soviet leaders were able to defeat the *kulaks*, to organize and direct the new industrial concerns, to handle the five-year plans skillfully. The real cost paid by the U.S.S.R. for forced industrialization was not the rise of a bourgeois capitalist class. To avoid that pitfall, the Soviets fell into its opposite: the rise

116

of what Djilas appropriately calls "a new class," an omnipotent, arrogant, dictatorial bureaucracy, which, in turn, generated a monster bureaucratic state.

Certainly, the most clear-minded Soviet leaders had foreseen the danger. But Stalin did not; or, better, he was the boss of the bureaucracy, its "identification model." So, forced industrialization was achieved, but the U.S.S.R. fell under the hegemony of a new class which, as a matter of fact, robbed industrial and farm laborers of what should have been "their" state.[8]

After the second world war, a similar process of forced industrialization was started in Communist China. To the superficial observer, the events that followed suggested that the Chinese were not quite sane: agrarian *commons*, backyard blast furnaces, "cultural revolution." What was concealed behind this façade? The Chinese revolution, in contrast with the Soviet upheaval, was overwhelmingly a peasants' revolution, with power firmly clenched in agrarian hands. The shrewd Chinese leaders did not want industrialization to be achieved at the cost of the rise of a "new class" of bureaucrats, which would have wrestled power from agrarian leaders; and, obviously, they did not want the rise of a bourgeois capitalist class either. They tried, therefore, to achieve forced industrialization by "slowing down," by giving preeminence to consumer goods over heavy industry (but not always); in any case, they tried to keep the entire process under the steady grasp of the agrarian class. Certainly, Chinese yeomen had to pay in part the cost of industrialization, but they, in the main, were willing to do this, as any class that exerts hegemony is surely willing to sacrifice something, provided that power would remain in its hands. The "apparatus" mainly used by Chinese leaders, as far as we can judge, is the People's Army, which is overwhelmingly composed of the peasantry.

We have stressed such examples in order to clearly focus on what the Confederacy had to face. First of all, and paramount: forced industrialization; second, prevalence of heavy (war) industry; third, speed, a speed that had to be far superior to that of both Russia and China. The positive refusal by the planter class to yield to a new bourgeoisie meant there was even the need of finding an "apparatus" to handle the enormous state-owned (or state-controlled) industrial concern that was about to rise, the Confederacy lacking, obviously, "organic" bourgeois managers. Certainly, Confederate leaders had no plans, no examples to follow, no guidelines. They had to proceed stumbling, like blind men exploring a new terrain. Nevertheless, what they achieved, the creative solutions that sprang from bare necessity, was amazing.

The first problem to deal with was, of course, capital investment. Where was the Confederacy to find capital to invest? This was possibly its weakest point, since, similar to Communist China, the ruling class was agrarian, and they could not, unlike Soviet Russia, become the victims of such a process.

The very lack of means of payment had dictated early Confederate policy to find monetary capital: "Without military stores; without the workshops to create them, without the power to import them," as President Davis wrote,[9] there was nothing but to ask the people to help the country as in the direst emergency. Truly, the Confederate Congress had approved on February 28, 1861, "An Act to raise Money for the support of the Government of the Confederate States of America";[10] in this Act, loans were indicated as the most immediate course to be followed, and, under it, a first public loan of $15 million was floated on March 16, 1861. This was soon followed by others, which joined the first $500,000 given to the Confederate government by the state of Alabama.

Later in 1861 the Confederate government turned toward what looked easier in an agrarian country where currency (for the time being!) was scarce: produce loans. A produce loan entailed a straightforward appeal to the patriotism of the planter class. In the mind of Secretary of the Treasury Christopher G. Memminger, the loans would act as a brake on a feared inflation by enabling the government to pay for supplies in loan bonds instead of currency.[11] All in all, the planter class showed a remarkable patriotism and understanding of its duties: "Subscriptions ranged from one-fourth to offers of the whole crop, and there were instances in which subscriptions were to remain in effect yearly during the course of war." [12] Encouraged by such an impressive response, the government soon floated another loan intended to raise the produce loan to $100 million. This second loan was to be compulsory, founded on a war tax on property, payable in gold, silver, Treasury notes, or raw produce.[13] The economic sensibility of the planters, this time, early saw what was to be the inevitable outcome of such an economic policy. From several sources, the government was urged to buy the whole crop on the basis of the average price of the last five years. Herschel W. Johnson, writing to James H. Hammond, tersely stated the issue, underlining that "king cotton would have performed its true function in the war only by Government management." [14]

Consequently, the most sensible segment of the planter class drew the obvious conclusion: only a state economy, based on nationalization of foreign trade, would give the government the means it needed. Remarkable in itself, the position also demonstrated that the planters understood this was the only way the Confederacy could wage war without putting itself in the hands of both local and foreign capitalists. However, the government—mainly Secretary Memminger—was not yet ready for such a policy. For the time being, it was considering the use of cotton for political, not economic, purposes. But withholding cotton exports, the government hoped to create a cotton famine in Great Britain and France and thus compel those powers to intervene by breaking the northern blockade. This, in time, turned out to be a major mistake. Indeed, the warehouses of Great Britain and France were clogged with cotton and, for the time being, did not move. In 1862, when their cotton reserves were exhausted, the federal blockade had been tightened. It was then that the Confederate government began to understand that cotton, although far from being a political tool, would have been instead the most precious asset of the Confederacy if it had been used to pay for purchases and agents abroad.

So, for the time being, the Confederate Treasury did not follow the planters' suggestion. As far as loans were concerned, the produce loan was first extended to $250 million and then followed by a series of loans and by the successful Erlanger loan, which yielded $15 million (almost $7 million net). Recourse to foreign credit was made, in the form of cotton certificates, to be sold abroad for £1,000 each. At the end of the war, the funded debt of the Confederate States of America amounted to $712,046,420.[15]

Apart from loans, at the beginning of the war the Confederate government had very small monetary reserves, about $389,267 in specie. Throughout the country the banks had about $26 million more, which, of course, formed their reserves and could not be seized. Schwab wrote that, throughout the war, the Confederate government succeeded in getting about $27 million in species.[16] Since this was, of course, quite insufficient, monetary capital had to be found elsewhere.

A complete appraisal of the investments made by the Confederate government throughout the war to create an industrial organization *ex nihilo* has never been done, as far as I know. Certainly, as the inclusive cost of the war (not calculating destruction of property and lives) to the Confederacy amounted to about $4 billion,[17] the yield of loans was not enough, even though the planter class, which contributed the blood of its sons, also gave willingly large amounts of money.

Another way to raise capital was by taxation. But the Confederate Congress was unwilling to do this. To tax the poor would have been not only egotistical but utterly foolish and totally ruinous. To tax the rich would have alienated the ruling agrarian class, the class on which the Confederacy was founded.

Nevertheless, as President Davis insisted, the Congress did resort to taxation on imports. Since the Confederate Constitution forbade any tariff for protective purposes, the government limited the levy to moderate duties for revenue purposes only. Although the need for an income tax began to appear, the Confederate Congress was again unwilling to make that commitment. Finally, however, repeated pressure from Secretary Memminger convinced the Congress to create, on February 25, 1863, an indirect tax of 8 percent on agricultural products and naval stores held on July 1, 1863, and retroactive to the 1862 crop, with a deduction for articles for home consumption. The same 8 percent tax was extended to any kind of money, including bank notes and deposits not used in business, with the exception of credits held abroad which were to be taxed at 1 percent. Intended to hit speculation profits, a 10 percent tax was placed on profits resulting from trade, excluding retail business, in 1862. A license tax was put on a series of businesses, its rate varying according to the expected profits. A progressive income tax was levied on net incomes, which, after an exemption of $1,000, rose from 1 percent on the first $1,500 to 2 percent (this rate was applied only to wages; for profits other than wages, the rate was stiffer, from 5 percent on incomes between $500 and $1,500 to 15 percent on incomes over $15,000). Later, a tax in kind was added of 10 percent of the agricultural product grown in 1863.[18] In 1864 the Tax Act was modified in order to add several more percentages. Totally, by means of tariffs and taxes, the Confederacy collected, throughout its life, $207,515,333.13.

Aside from specie reserves, loans, and taxes, the Confederacy had one more means to create its "primary accumulation": the printing press—or inflation. A careful study of Memminger's, Davis's, and George Trenholm's papers shows clearly, in my mind, that no Confederate leader ever willingly considered inflation as a means to raise money. Rather, they saw clearly how inflation was prejudicial to the Confederate cause.[19] However, the Confederacy decided soon to issue Treasury notes, an act, in itself, wholly natural, as the Confederacy needed paper money as a circulating medium. However, as soon as the expenses of the Confederacy proved enormous, beyond any possibility of being covered either by loans or by taxes, the printing press went ahead steadily. By the end, the Confederacy had put into circulation $1,554,087,354 in Treasury notes; in the same period, the general price index, at 100 in January 1861, had skyrocketed, as far as the southeastern states were concerned, through April 1865 to 9211.[20] This meant discharging the cost of forced industrialization upon the people at large, the usual result of inflation. Inflation, in turn, would have conjured up a tremendous capitalist class, as Thermidorean inflation did in revolutionary France, unless the industrial policy of Confederate authorities had made such a rise all but impossible.

Scholars have spent years and floods of ink researching the real cause of Confederate inflation. Since it was not a deliberate policy of the government, the question is: why did it occur? Let us look for a moment at the North during the war to attempt a hypothesis deserving of further research. As far as public debt was concerned, the Union government, in 1861, had a total debt of $90,582,000; in August 1965, the debt had reached $2,846,000,000. The amount caused by inflation (i.e., issuance of paper money, legal tender, so-called greenbacks) totaled $589,000,000. The rate of inflation that hit the north, then, was smaller than that plaguing the South. Consequently, northern inflation was, conforming with capitalist interests, a "healthy inflation," intended to act as a stimulus on an economy strong enough to draw benefits from it (at least, benefits to the capitalist class). The price index to consumers (1858 = 100), which was 102 in 1861, did not go beyond 177 in 1865.[21]

In other words, whereas the main source of financing in the South was inflation, in the North it was loans.[22] So the North presented the aspect, soon to become characteristic, of a large, strong industrial community at war: the government mobilized savings and invested them in war manufacturing, increasing enormously the business, profits—and power—of capitalists. The Union certainly had a tremendous cost to pay, but its task did not go beyond setting its economy on a war footing. Whereas the Confederacy, before putting its industries to work, had to meet the appalling cost of "primary accumulation" to create such industries from nothing. This was too much of an effort, and inflation was the consequence. However, southern inflation was far different from northern inflation. Instead of being a "healthy" spur to the economy in order to stimulate it (and increase capitalists' profits), southern inflation amounted to no less than a true expropriation of a community and did not enrich any particular private group. It gave only the measure of the sacrifices that the whole agrarian southern community was ready to face in order to industrialize—and remain agrarian. Only victory in the field would have solved the problem; but, after all, who could say that this southern, quasi-socialist utopia was not doomed to defeat from its very beginnings?

At any rate, the southern effort was an imposing one. Let us take a summary view of it: first, the private industrial sector, under government control; then, the public, or national, sector; and last, how the Confederacy, which had no party or bureaucratic "apparatus," managed to handle such a mighty effort.

When the Confederacy was founded, it relied first, for its defense, on captured federal weapons.[23] These were absolutely not enough, even if, in many cases, they gave an early substantial boost to the southern cause (for example, the heavy guns captured at Norfolk by the navy). Armaments were also purchased abroad. However, it very soon appeared clear that no war might be waged without a powerful home industry.

To begin with, the Confederate government acted immediately to nationalize the whole productive power of existing manufactures as far as war production was concerned. First and foremost was the famous Tredegar Iron Works of Richmond, where the owner, J. R. Anderson (possibly foreseeing the industrial policy of the Confederate government), urged the Confederacy to take over his business. The offer was not accepted for the time being, as Confederate authorities were content to enlist the Tredegar's whole production for the war economy.[24]

Following the Tredegar, practically every other existing industry was put under contract by the government. This was the first step. However, Confederate authorities did more, suggesting to any willing entrepreneur that he start a new industrial business. Although in many cases these were nothing more than individual artisan shops, large plants were also thus stimulated. Such enterprises had to be encouraged and the government helped by lending 50 percent of the setting up expenses and advancing as much as one-third of the value of the contemplated output. This, obviously, gave the government the upper hand over such private firms. To begin with, such industries were allowed to produce only for the government, and second, the profits of such industries were first limited by law to 75 percent, then reduced to 33.5 percent, to keep prices on a reasonable level. Prospective profits had to be calculated on the basis of production costs. Confederate authorities soon discovered, however, that many contractors inflated costs in order to increase their share of profits. The government took the next step and imposed fixed prices. However, the sharp rise of prices because of inflation necessitated the creation of arbitration commissions with the task of modifying prices periodically.

However, such industries were totally under government rule, which was strengthened by the use of two tools forcefully handled by the Confederate authorities. First, universal conscription permitted designation of skilled workmen for industrial needs and, second, the war economy was enforced by putting (too late, it is true) rail transportation under public control. The government, therefore, was able to make industrialists obedient to its will by refusing to detail men or to allow transportation facilities to firms that did not conform to the stringent regulations.

As far as textile mills were concerned, the Confederate authorities, which had allowed such plants duty-free imports of textile machinery for the duration of war, were able to intervene effectively. Having a quasi-monopoly of cotton, they could withhold raw materials from industrialists who did not conform completely to national discipline.[25] Civilians soon discovered that having wool carded at any factory was all but impossible except with the consent of the authorities, as the government had all factories under its control.[26] Among the largest private factories under the government's control were the famous textile plants of Graniteville, South Carolina, owned by William Gregg, who in 1863 signed a contract for 100,000 yards of sheeting, computed by the authorities at $43,020.[27] "By spring 1863 . . . John Pemberton's 30,000 troops defending Vicksburg were able to exist 'almost exclusively' on clothing and equipment manufactured in Mississippi." [28] The Tredegar Iron Works were producing their full capacity under contract. They turned out ordnance, ordnance stores, railroad equipment and rails, plates for ironclads, and machinery for warships.

Joseph R. Anderson, the capable manager (who had been made a general in the Confederate service), agreed to alter his rolling mill so as to be able to turn out two-inch iron plates for the famous, first Confederate ironclad, the *Virginia*.[29]

In all, the South had ten more rolling mills, several of which were small.[30] Six were able to turn out only 1 to 400 tons of bar iron. The Atlanta Rolling Mill did not produce bar iron, but could make a small amount of railroad track; under government contract, it altered its equipment and by December 1861 was able to produce 150 iron plates a day, destined for the tremendous ironclad, the *Mississippi*, under construction at New Orleans. The Etowah Iron Works of Rome, Georgia, was put under contract to produce heavy cannon, shot, and shells.[31]

In addition to the small plants, the Confederacy had another factory able to roll plates for ironclads: the Shelby Iron Company of Alabama, which was soon put under contract to deliver its entire production of 12,000 tons per year to the government.[32] The navy, however, received an unsatisfactory share of plates, mainly the result of an iron shortage. Secretary Mallory, at any rate, had more satisfaction from another firm, the Bellona Iron Works of Richmond, Virginia, which was put under contract to supply cannon, both rifled and smoothbore.

All of the thirty-nine furnaces existing in the Confederacy were put to work for the government. Iron ore, however, soon began to run short. The government advanced funds for building more furnaces, and between 1862 and 1863, thirteen new furnaces were built in Alabama and fifteen in Virginia, and the government kept stringent control over them all. It even had (as we shall see later) its own foundries. However, to own foundries was one thing, to supply them with iron ore, quite another. So, the Confederate authorities had to rely more and more on railroad iron, which certainly did not help solve the terrible transportation problem, even if the government tried to take over the iron from "needless trunks." Several of these privately owned government-controlled factories sprang up for the needs of war and had no life outside government contracts; such was the Cook & Brother Armory of Athens, Georgia, which was able to produce up to 600 rifles per month.[33]

As far as internal transportation was concerned, the Confederacy had to face an appalling situation. Many trainmen were northerners who, after secession, went back home, deserting their posts. Material was scarce; two northern railroad companies had half as many passenger cars and as many engines as the whole Confederacy.[34] Among the worst causes of southern collapse was the breakdown of the railroad system. The government tried to assume control, first putting the superintendent of the Wilmington and Weldon Railroad, then that of the New Orleans, Jackson and Great Northern in office as directors of the railroads, but they were able to accomplish little. Only on May 1, 1863, did the Confederate authorities act with customary energy. Colonel F. M. Sims of the Quartermaster Department was placed in charge of railroads with ample power, which enabled him to improve the service. Then, on February 28, 1865, the Congress decided on a wholesale take-over, putting all kinds of transportation, including railroads, steamboats, and canals, along with communications (telegraph lines), under the direct control of the Secretary of War and appropriating $21 million for the rehabilitation of the railroads. But it was too late. One can only wonder what would have followed such a practical take-over by the government of the entire railroad network.[35]

Certainly, such ironhanded control by national authorities of the private sector of industry and transportation allowed the industrialists only small profits, even if people were speaking wildly of enormous gains. Profits assuredly existed; however, it was also true that industrialists feared, more than they wanted, government contracts, as they usually had to produce at a loss or with very small earnings.[36] At any rate, inflation soon leveled profits; in contrast to the North (only logical, being a capitalist country), in the South no industrialist made his fortune through war profits.

Having firmly established its control over manufacturing and transportation, the Confederacy took the next and most important step: the creation of a wide, nationally owned industrial sector. The first, obvious decision to be made was to put to work the existing arsenals; but the Confederacy did more: eight arsenals were transformed into large armories (Richmond,

Fayetteville, Augusta, Charleston, Columbus, Macon, Atlanta, Selma); three smaller arsenals (Danville, Lynchburg, and Montgomery) were put to work at their maximum capacity. In a short time, armories began mass production. The Richmond Ordnance Laboratory turned out from 50,000 to 100,000 rounds of small-arms ammunition and 900 rounds of artillery ammunition daily. The Richmond Armory produced 1,000 small arms per month; the Fayetteville Armory, up to 500 small arms per month; the big Augusta Armory, 20,000 to 30,000 rounds of small-arms cartridges daily; the Charleston Armory, 15,000 to 20,000 daily; the Baton Rouge Arsenal (before it was lost to the enemy), 30,000 to 40,000.[37]

This was in 1861. Later, the Richmond Armory reached a production rate of 5,000 small arms per month, the largest in the Confederacy. The Richmond Ordnance Laboratory began to produce percussion caps, cartridges, rockets, hand grenades, gun carriages, even 12-pounder Napoleons, small arms, and canteens. In addition, the Richmond Laboratory produced more than a million percussion caps during the war.[38] In 1862 the production in eight nationally owned armories had skyrocketed to 170,000 cartridges and 1,000 field-artillery rounds of ammunitions daily and 155,000 pounds of lead monthly.[39]

Very soon the Confederacy began to fear a shortage of powder. To eliminate the danger, Confederate authorities organized what resulted in one of their most amazing national plants: the giant Augusta Powder Works at Augusta, Georgia. The buildings of the old United States Magazine were taken and the land around them purchased. Through the genius of Colonel George W. Rains, who, by means of only a pamphlet summarily describing the process and machinery in use at the largest plant in the world, the big Waltham Abbey Powder Works in England, succeeded in building a Confederate plant, from warehouses to machines. The Augusta Powder Works, whose tremendous chimney still stands near the silent canal to testify to the rise and fall of the largest nationally owned factory system in the world to that time, soon began production. It bypassed Waltham Abbey and was able to produce 2,750,000 pounds of powder throughout the war. The capital investment of the

Confederate government to build such a tremendous works amounted to the small sum of $385,000.[40] Minor powder mills were created at San Antonio, Texas, and Petersburg, Virginia, where a lead-smelting factory, nationally owned, was also organized.[41]

Confederate military factories needed lead, copper, iron, niter, and zinc. To provide such raw material, the Niter and Mining Bureau was created, which later had to also supply coal mines. The bureau soon put many plants under its tight control, including the small plants roasting pyrites to produce sulfur and any existing mine; it even organized its own factories, creating, country-wide, hundreds of niter beds. By the end of 1864 there were almost one million cubic feet of such niter beds in operation.[42] The bureau also took charge of the nationally owned lead-smelting works at Petersburg. A sizable cannon foundry was created at Macon, Georgia, to produce heavy guns; another for shot and shells at Salisbury, North Carolina; and three bronze foundries at Macon, Columbus, and Augusta, Georgia.

The army also organized ". . . a large shop for leather-works at Clarksville, Virginia . . . ; at Fayetteville . . . a manufactory of carbines; a rifle factory at Asheville (transferred to Columbia, South Carolina); a new and very large armory at Macon, including a pistol factory; a second pistol factory at Columbus, Ga." And the man who directed this gigantic effort could well remark: "Where ten years ago we were not making a gun, a pistol nor a sabre, no shot nor shell (except at the Tredegar Works)—a pound of powder—we now make all these in quantities to meet the demands of our large Armies." [43]

He was, indeed, right. Never before in history had anything like this been seen. A backward agricultural country, with only small, truly preindustrial plants, had created a gigantic industry, investing millions of dollars, arming and supplying one of the largest armies in the world—and all this as national property or under national control, in a kind of quasi-socialist management. Not even the spectacular industrialization of Soviet Russia, which allowed it to field a tremendous army of tanks, heavy guns, and airplanes to defeat Nazi Germany, was to be so impressive, since Russia would be allowed more than ten years and a state of peace in which to accomplish it, while the Confederacy was allowed fewer than four years, complicated by the strain of war.

A conspicuous part of the new, nationally owned industrial plants sprang up on the initiative of the navy. The Confederacy was not a naval power. Even before the war, cotton had been shipped abroad in northern vessels, and slaves imported by northern shipping. Of the 8,000 vessels of any size and description built in the United States between 1849 and 1858, only 1,600 had been built in the South, and these were, for the most part, small craft for river or coastal navigation.[44] The Confederate states possessed only two navy yards, Norfolk, Virginia, and Pensacola, Florida, and the latter had been mainly a coaling station.[45] Moreover, it was soon blockaded by the presence of federals at Fort Pickens. The 1860 Census enumerated thirty-six privately owned shipyards throughout the Confederacy, but many were small, able to put together only barges or something similar.

With unconquerable energy, any existing shipyard was put to work for the navy; new Navy yards were created at New Orleans, Louisiana, and Memphis, Tennessee. In 1862 both cities were lost to the enemy, together with Norfolk and Pensacola. The navy had to start anew. And it did. New navy yards were built at Richmond (the "Rocketts"); Edward's Ferry and Whitehall, North Carolina; Mars Bluff, South Carolina; Safford and Columbus, Georgia; Yazoo City, Mississippi; Selma, Montgomery, and Owen Bluff, Alabama; and Shreveport, Louisiana. The biggest part of such yards was nationally owned.[46] Some were created absolutely *ex nihilo*, in what had been, in the case of Edward's Ferry, a cornfield.

To meet the problem of marine machinery, the Navy Department bought and put to work the Shockoe Foundry at Richmond, Virginia, and another large plant for producing engine parts, shafts, propellers, and anchors was created at Charlotte, North Carolina. But the greatest factory grew up at Columbus, Georgia, where the navy bought the Columbus Iron Works, a small plant like the Shockoe Foundry, and, as they did at Shockoe, transformed it by enlarging it and adding a rolling mill and a boiler plant. In time, the Columbus Iron Works became the largest factory in the Confederacy for manufacturing marine machinery.[47] The navy even created a large rope walk at Petersburg, Virginia, which was able to supply in full the needs for cordage of any description.

Among the greatest national industries organized by the navy was, undoubtedly, the Selma Cannon Foundry. Like other plants, it had begun as a private venture; however, it soon was realized that private capitalists were not able to produce in a satisfactory way without heavy losses. Consequently, in June 1863 the foundry was bought by the navy and transformed into a most important plant to cast heavy ordnance; to the end of the war, more than one hundred enormous naval cannon were cast at Selma.[48] After the fall of Norfolk and New Orleans, another new factory was established at Charlotte, North Carolina, to manufacture gun carriages, shot, percussion caps, and other ordnance stores; another ordnance plant was organized in Richmond; and a third in Atlanta. The navy even had its own Powder Works in Columbia, South Carolina.

In all, the navy created twenty shipyards, five ordnance plants, two marine machinery works, and one powder mill.[49] The Confederate navy, from 1861 to 1865, "converted, contracted for or laid down within its [Confederate] borders at least 150 warships." [50] Possibly the most amazing ships were the ironclads, of which the Confederacy built twenty-two, while at least thirty more were laid down or contracted for.[51] One has only to remember that in 1861 the Confederacy was utterly unable even to dream of building an ironclad to recognize the accomplishment. It did have the raw materials—ore inside the earth and trees in southern forests. To build ironclads, it was necessary to begin by creating, from nothing, the industry able to make them.

To conclude, in the Confederacy there existed another productive sector, which was neither completely national nor private under national control. To manufacture cloth, the Confederacy put up a large factory in Richmond, which was, of course, nationally owned. But it only cut the cloth, which was then distributed to about two thousand women who manufactured uniforms in their homes; in Atlanta, another similar plant put to work three thousand women, sewing uniforms.[52] So the Confederacy resurrected old-fashioned home industries, which had been popular at the dawn of the capitalist age. However, now the housewife was not managed by mercantile capitalists, but by the government, which was both owner and manager. For other parts of uniforms, the government organized totally nationally owned factories. A large brass-button factory was created in Atlanta and shoe factories in Richmond (800 pairs a day), Columbus, Georgia (5,000 pairs a week), and Atlanta (1,300 pairs daily during the first month).[53]

What is worth observing is that the Confederacy, by organizing its national industry, tended to create big industrial cities, in which the most important national plants were located, whereas the private ones under public control were usually (with exceptions) in smaller localities. Among the most remarkable of such industrial cities was Richmond, which, near the famous Tredegar and another privately owned plant, the Bellona Iron Works, had a navy yard, a large armory, an ordnance laboratory, a marine machinery workshop, a cloth factory, and several minor ventures.

Augusta, Georgia, was truly a "Confederate city."[54] Near the gigantic Confederate Powder Works, the nation owned a large arsenal, a bronze foundry, navy grinding mills, meat-packing plants, and a factory to produce uniforms, clothing, and shoes for naval personnel. Here the navy possessed "an invaluable labor-saving machine made in England that cut leather and cloth in quantities so large that one man could do the work of fifty."[55]

Columbus, Georgia, had a great armory, a pistol factory, and a navy yard, together with the large Naval Iron Works and Rolling Mill, a bronze foundry, and a shoe factory.[56] Atlanta had a great Confederate arsenal, a navy ordnance plant, a rolling mill, and a shoe factory. Macon, Georgia, had a heavy-cannon foundry, a bronze foundry, a large armory with a pistol factory, all nationally owned. Selma, Alabama, besides the famous Naval Foundry, had a navy yard, which built three great ironclads, and a large arsenal, employing more than 10,000 persons. All these establishments were nationally owned.[57] Such major industrial centers tended to evolve into true "concerns." Had the Confederacy lasted a little longer, coordination of national productive activities in such centers would have brought more and more planning and centralization—whether for better or for worse, nobody can say. At any rate, this is a problem transcending the limits of this book.

To be sure, the privately owned sector, even if under national control (and most probably because of this), tended to shrink, at least as far as the major plants were concerned. Private capitalism cannot grow and prosper under such a regime; consequently, one after another, private firms were bought out by the Confederacy in what amounted to a true process of nationalization. The Bibb Iron Company in Alabama was purchased "because the owners refused to comply with governmental regulations." [58] Others followed: the great Selma Cannon Foundry, the Shockoe Foundry, several shipyards, the Columbus Iron Works. Even Joseph R. Anderson, owner of what was called the big Tredegar "empire," found himself in the clutches of a crisis in late 1864. In despair, he tried every way to proceed, from borrowing to barter. Reluctantly, he proposed that the government take over the business. Because the government esteemed the patriotic behavior of Anderson, who was a Confederate brigadier general, it refused the offer. But here, too, the question arises. Had the Confederacy lasted longer, would it have been able to go ahead without nationalizing even the Tredegar, obviously keeping the able Anderson as a manager? [59]

In 1864 the Confederacy was the owner of a tremendous industry. The private sector, which was all but fading away, was coming more and more under stringent government control. This situation foretold the next step, for the Confederacy was about to adopt another basic characteristic of a socialist economy: the nationalization of foreign trade.

11

Transportation and the Nationalization of Foreign Trade

Had he been allowed to do so by the Legislature, President Davis would have placed more stringent control over railroads than that decided on by Congress; at any rate, it was the government that took the initiative of completing the railroad network for strategic purposes.

The worst gap in southern railroads was that between Danville, Virginia, and Greensboro, North Carolina. In November 1861 President Davis clearly warned the Congress that the Confederacy had to solve this problem, as private initiative could not be trusted. Indeed, private initiative (which still owned the railroads) delayed the solution. It was not until May 1864 that trains were able to roll on the new tracks linking the Confederate north to the Confederate south—just in time, for the other two lines were then being broken by the enemy. In 1862 President Davis had been able to close another gap, between Selma, Alabama, and Meridian, Mississippi. But already stressed, the insistence of President Davis on putting all the railroads under national control was not fully successful until too late.[1]

However, as far as foreign trade was concerned, false steps would have been exceedingly dangerous, as the northern blockade was becoming tighter and tighter. In the meantime, the enormous profits to be made by buying cotton in the Confederacy at 6 to 10 cents a pound and selling it in Europe at 50 to 60 had attracted a swarm of blockade-runners, mainly English, who created a brisk trade between the Confederacy and the Bahamas, Bermuda, and even Mexico.[2]

Certainly, such businessmen (some of them northerners, who loved their pocketbooks far more than their country) were not running the blockade out of any enthusiasm for the Confederate cause, but only for the sake of making a lot of fast and relatively easy money. Why should they have crammed their holds with war supplies, which were heavy, cumbersome, and dangerous? The best goods to sell in the South were those of small dimension, little weight, and a high price per pound. Instead of bringing in powder, shot, shells, cartridges, rifles, and cannon, blockade-runners preferred to swamp the South with French perfume, wine, liquor, champagne, silk, and satin. Even southern-owned firms joined the lucrative trade.[3] It became quickly evident that, even in such a delicate sector, the Confederacy could not trust private capitalism, neither the well-established European and Yankee entrepreneurs nor the speculative southern newcomers.

To forestall an ominous situation, the Confederate government tried, in a rather disorganized and haphazard way, to launch its own blockade-runners. First, Captain James Bulloch had made his memorable trip in the fall of 1861 aboard the *Fingal*. By bringing in some 10,000 excellent Enfield rifles, 1 million cartridges, 2 million percussion caps, 400 barrels of powder, and much other manifold weaponry, Bulloch demonstrated what the Confederates might have achieved had they directly managed their own blockade-runners.[4] On his side, the clever General Josiah Gorgas, chief of the Ordnance Bureau, managed to have his own blockade-runners, and in a short time his bureau possessed five vessels, which ran the blockade exclusively at the service of the Ordnance and Quartermaster departments.[5] The Navy Department, too, had its own vessels, as did some states, such as North Carolina, which owned the famous steamer *Ad-Vance*, so named in honor of its governor's wife.[6]

But this was certainly not enough. Captain Bulloch had already urged the Secretary of the Navy to nationalize the blockade-running business.[7] In the fall of 1863 the government took the first step, compelling the owners of ships running the blockade to put one-third to one-half of their holds at the disposition of Confederate authorities. The results were dismaying: freight rates skyrocketed from $300 to $1,000 per ton.[8] It was clear that nothing short of the nationalization of foreign trade would work. Shortly, General Colin J. McRae was appointed financial agent for Europe, with the task of taking charge of administering Confederate funds abroad and of centralizing any purchasing or disbursing operation.[9] Both Captain Bulloch and the able Confederate agent for propaganda abroad, Henry Hotze, supported McRae in recommending the cancellation of any private contract and the take-over of foreign trade by the Confederate government.

At last, on February 6, 1864, President Davis took two definite steps. Under his strong encouragement, the Congress approved two laws: the first forbade any further importation of luxuries; the second prohibited the export of cotton, tobacco, military and naval stores, sugar, molasses, and rice, except under special regulations to be made by the President.[10] The regulations stipulated that ships exporting any quantity of the above quoted commodities (i.e., mainly cotton) were required to put one-half of their holds—either in outbound or homeward trips—at the disposition of Confederate authorities. Freight rates were strictly fixed and compulsory; the half-hold that remained at the owners' disposition had to carry goods not forbidden by Confederate laws. Shipment of flammables, which might have endangered the government's freight, was kept strictly under government control and needed its authorization; ships had to submit lists of officers, crew, and passengers, who had to have regular passports; and cargoes had to be inspected by revenue officers.[11]

The main item the Confederacy might export was cotton. Consequently, the Confederate government took charge of collecting all cotton to be exported and appointed a special agent, Colonel Thomas L. Bayne, as chairman of the new bureau. With a congressional appropriation of $20,000,000, the bureau had the task of centralizing all cotton purchases and of shipping it exclusively in the name of the Confederate government. Bayne proved as efficient as McRae, and in a few months all Confederate trade was in the energetic hands of the two agents, one on each side of the Atlantic. Colonel Bayne also had the duty of choosing the more opportune ports of entry for blockade-runners and of accumulating stocks of cotton in each of them. As trans-Mississippi had been severed from the main body of the Confederacy, another agent, P. W. Gray, was appointed there.[12] Those ships that refused to accept Confederate regulations received no more products to export and were denied clearance papers.

In Europe, General McRae, under Confederate instructions, continued to nationalize Confederate foreign trade: he bought four excellent blockade-runners and had ten more laid down. When the Confederacy fell, six blockade-runners were already sailing between Europe and America. Other arrangements, made either by Bulloch or McRae, were intended to bring the Confederate nationally owned merchant marine up to twenty-seven steamers, the greatest government-owned fleet of traders prior to the nationalized Soviet fleet.[13] In the meantime, Confederate agents in Europe were speeding up the building of war vessels, intended for breaking the blockade.

The nationalization of foreign trade soon yielded handsome results. Confederate credit in Europe began to rise: the Erlanger's Bonds, which, after Vicksburg and Gettysburg, had fallen to 42, rose to 77 in August 1864. By December, the government had already exported cotton worth $5,296,606 (equivalent to $132,500,000 in Confederate notes). Unpublished as well as printed records show that the federal blockade, however effective, was broken more frequently in 1864–65 than any time previously. This, in spite of violent opposition from several states, such as Georgia and North Carolina, which operated their own blockade-running business and tried in every way to torpedo Confederate plans. Although they did not succeed, they created a considerable headache for central authorities.

Certainly, the Confederate government was going boldly

against the time-honored doctrine of states' rights, but what else might it have done? All in all, it is a wonder how much states' rights were respected in the Confederacy: the South was trying to fight its war without reneging on its cherished principles.[14] It is amazing to see how many southern ideals were respected, with the exception of President Davis's application of the principle *salus populi suprema lex esto.*

In the meantime, nationalized trade was sailing with favorable winds. However, as Louise B. Hill observed, this plan had been entered into too late. The Confederacy was being defeated, and not, as the legend still maintains, because of the blockade. Simplifying the issue, one might surmise that the basic cause of defeat was, rather, the breakdown of the Confederate railway system, which was responsible for the starvation of Lee's army, when Georgia, for instance, had plenty of food. If this be true, it follows that the principal cause of collapse came from the sector that had been put under public control imperfectly or too late.

So, through tremendous, almost superhuman effort, the Confederacy succeeded in fighting a total war against a highly industrialized and technologically advanced foe. And by means of the most sweeping experience in state socialism to that time, it succeeded in keeping the new industrialism under the iron control of a political class sprung up from an agrarian planter civilization. But another, perhaps even more amazing, aspect must be considered. As stressed earlier, any capitalist country has a vast array of "organic intellectuals"—businessmen, industrial capitalists, technicians, economists, managers—to handle its enormous technological concern. Three generations later, Soviet Russia had, as its tool, party bureaucracy. The Confederacy had nothing. How did it succeed in handling its enormous new industrial, financial, and trading organism? In other words, how did it handle its "socialist" economy? This is an interesting problem, one which, so far (at least it seems to me), has scarcely attracted the attention of historians.

The so-called developing countries of today, which, for the most part, are trying to emerge from an old-fashioned, agrarian, colonial status through a more or less forced industrialization, are accomplishing their aims in two ways. Either they take the road of capitalist industrialization, and in such cases, as John C. Calhoun had tersely foreseen,[15] they fall under the spell of foreign capitalism, which ties them permanently to a quasi-colonial status. Or they try to industrialize by keeping as much of their independence as they can. The most prominent country to follow this second road is contemporary China. At its beginnings, like Yugoslavia, Communist China relied mainly on Soviet "help." Soon it realized it was simply following the path of the countries that were falling prey to foreign capitalism. On the very brink of becoming a colony of a state-capitalist country, not of a private-capitalist one, China and many other "developing countries" followed a different path. As they had neither a foreign nor a national capitalist apparatus, and did not want a large bureaucracy, they relied upon the army to handle their economy—even, in some cases, to start their revolutions. This, of course, happened in various and different degrees, but, as a rule, army men had the task of supplying the personnel to direct national industries and planning.

What is amazing is that one hundred years ago the Confederacy did the same thing. Certainly, what it did sprang from the necessity of war, but it is still cause for wonder how the Confederacy managed to raise an "apparatus" of competent, energetic, honest officers who took the place of the lacking capitalist and technocratic managers. The most prominent among them was possibly General Josiah Gorgas, chief of the Confederate Ordnance Bureau; with him worked both General George W. Rains, chief of the Niter and Mining Bureau, and another extraordinary man, Colonel John W. Mallet, director of Chemistry, who was responsible for producing ammunitions and explosives. The energy of Gorgas, Mallet, and Rains conjured up, from almost nothing, industrial plants, put them to work, supplied them with raw materials and directed them. Among others, it will suffice to remember Commander John Mercer Brooke, chief of the navy's Bureau of Ordnance and Hydrography; Commander Catesby Jones, superintendent in chief of the big Selma Naval Foundry; Colonel James L. White, in charge of the Selma Arsenal; and a legion of officers, both from the army and navy, who managed the myriad arsenals, armories, foundries, ironworks, shipyards, and repair shops throughout the country. We should not forget the able agent in Europe, General Colin J. McRae; the chief of the Bureau of Foreign Supplies, Colonel Thomas L. Bayne; the navy's European agent, Commander William L. Bulloch; and many others. A study of this amazing managerial apparatus, which made Confederate national industry and trade going concerns without resorting to capitalist technocracy, would be of the deepest interest.

The Climax of Utopia: Confederate Emancipation

The first requisite for fighting total war is men. The Confederacy understood this well, and it passed and enforced the first conscription bill in America. Here, too, the Confederate government diverged sharply from well-established American tradition. At the end of the war, the most stringent conscription laws had been approved. After the first, another followed on February 17, 1864, when the Confederate Congress extended conscription to able-bodied males from seventeen to fifty years of age. Older and younger men were frequently required to serve in state militias.

Very early in the war the Confederacy felt a shortage of men. With only 5,581,298 free persons as against 21,527,268 inhabitants of the so-called free states, the Confederacy was hopelessly outnumbered. However, it had on its behalf the most basic motivation to raise armies and send men to fight and to die: the country had been invaded by a non-attacked foe; there was no other choice than to fight. But soon the Confederacy met one of the most appalling problems created by forced industrialization: the need of creating *ex nihilo* a working class. Soviet Russia, years later, would rely on farmers and yeomen transformed compulsorily into industrial workers; the Confederacy could not. Certainly, it had a reserve of 3,522,034 slaves, and from them came a tremendous number of intelligent, active factory workers. Nevertheless, the Confederacy lacked skilled labor and had to detail it from the army. This generated endless conflicts and wrangles, especially as the army was more and more outnumbered by the enemy in the field. In other words, the Confederacy found itself in a true shirt of Nessus: the shortage of labor was worsening; the Marietta (Georgia) Paper Mill had to close because of a lack of labor; [1] other plants were in distress.

The contribution of African slaves to the Confederate war effort has not yet been adequately studied. Very few scholars, for instance, have studied how many soldiers were spared for the firing line by African labor impressed by military authorities to build fortifications and engineering works. In the main, blacks were competent and amazingly loyal, their loyalty to the Confederacy indicating their understanding that the North was not fighting in their behalf, and it witnesses as well the political maturity of southerners of African origin.

The sophisticated Confederate political élite was not slow to understand these facts. Possibly, the problem of arming the slaves shows more than any other the high quality of the political class generated by southern civilization. That admirable man, President Jefferson Davis, can really be taken as the symbol of the seigneurial class at its best. One has only to read his argument for freeing the slaves and taking those who volunteered into the Confederate army to see once again how far-sighted, clear-minded he was. Much stress has been put on the bitter resistance that the emergency measure proposed by President Davis met: true, there were among southern planters many narrow-minded, egotistical men. As previously stated, a social class is most likely to be prone to egotistical private interests (even if, in many cases, slaveholders showed more independence than other ruling classes); but the final destiny of a civilization, its "historic" niche, is not settled by members of the social class but by those from the political sphere.

It is noteworthy that the movement to free the slaves and make of them comrades in arms of southern soldiers grew up in the Confederate army, after its first proposal appeared (according to Professor Durden) in a newspaper of the Deep South, pro-slavery state of Mississippi.[2] Alabama followed suit, and several eminent politicians began to think seriously about the matter. The problem of freeing the slaves, and making them citizens of the Confederacy provided they fought for it, was already being debated in Confederate newspapers, enrolling considerable public opinion in its behalf; and President Davis was beginning to move cautiously toward it when, in January 1864, General Patrick Cleburne, one of the ablest field commanders of the Confederacy and himself a landowner, wrote his famous letter to his colleagues proposing boldly to free the slaves and put them into the ranks. As the North was already arming the ex-slaves (in a way, let it be said, which showed that Union generals were more concerned with finding cannon fodder than in giving equality to the blacks), the South had to be able to do the same on an ampler basis, since the ex-slaves would be fighting for their homes and country.

Twelve other generals and Confederate officers of almost all ranks and states, among them several from prominent planter families, signed the letter together with Cleburne. As plainly visible in the records, the highest generals of the Army of Tennessee fully agreed. However, President Davis, a practical-minded man, considered Cleburne's scheme too grandiose (he spoke of arming 600,000 ex-slaves) and premature.[3]

But then, the President, encouraged by a large sector of public opinion, set steadily to work to achieve at least a partial emancipation of slave-soldiers. Soon an influential member of the seigneurial élite, General Lee himself, joined the President; Secretary of State Judah P. Benjamin sent a diplomatic mission to Europe offering to France and Great Britain emancipation in exchange for recognition. Certainly, it is all too easy to scorn the Confederacy because it offered emancipation when it was almost doomed: one has only to think that slaveholders were speaking of *their own* expropriation, and that very rarely in history has an exploiting class ever arrived at such a degree of intellectual independence and self-denial. Purely political ideals were almost predominating in the South; and this last deed by the seigneurial class was certainly among its most amazing.

In the end, President Davis prevailed and a bill to arm a portion of the slaves was approved by Congress; it did not contain any hint of emancipation, true, but emancipation was implicitly and clearly stated both by President Davis's and General Lee's declarations, and by the regulations for enrolling them into the army.[4] But what was more important, Confederate emancipation prevailed; it succeeded in gaining the approval of a majority of public opinion and a very large majority within the army.[5]

A comparison, as far as I know, of Davis's plan for emancipation and Lincoln's Proclamation with the Thirteenth Amendment has very rarely if ever been made. Lincoln's acts, important as they were, aimed to free a social class exploited by others than the group to which Lincoln belonged; whereas the Confederates were speaking of emancipating their own slaves and of hurting their own interests. Moreover, the 1862 Proclamation had been expressly intended as a confiscation act of a sort: as a matter of fact, it did not apply to loyal or already submitted slave states. As far as the Thirteenth Amendment is concerned, certainly Lincoln, had he lived, would have in some way compensated the South—with northern money. When he was assassinated, however, any project in this direction died with him. The South was abandoned to itself, and so were the blacks; the North did not want them.[6] The southern plan, instead, not only freed slave-soldiers, but also granted them southern citizenship and a homestead.[7]

In this way, thanks to Davis, Lee, and the most clear-minded members of the southern seigneurial class, not only the conduct of the war, industrialization, and trade was placed firmly in the hands of the agrarian class, but also emancipation. Indeed, emancipation was not to be conducted in a capitalist way—freeing the slaves to create a wide mass of jobless, homeless persons, ready to fill up the ranks of the "industrial reserve army" —but in a limited and gradual way, even, socially organized to help the integration of the new, black yeoman class into the existing social order, helping the planter civilization to survive, and (who knows?) even to be strengthened.

This was certainly a rather conservative—surely not a revolutionary—way to achieve emancipation, but neither was the northern proposal revolutionary, as no ruling class can be expected to commit suicide by organizing a revolution against itself. The southern way, however, would possibly have been more humane in comparison with the northern, certainly it would have been less demagogic and more solicitous even of the fate of the blacks by integrating them into a stable, harmonic society, paternally ruled by the seigneurial class.

This was the swan song of the seigneurial class. The "ideal state" was collapsing in ashes. It was indeed the end of a world— a world so far from us, so difficult to understand, endowed with paternalistic institutions, the patriarchal family, the predominance of country over town, the old-fashioned, preindustrial economy. It is extremely difficult with our own social-cultural conditioning to try to capture the peculiar flavor of such a civilization; certainly, it is utterly impossible to study it by applying to it the yardstick of our own civilization.

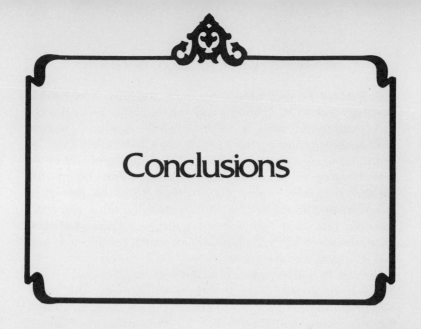

Conclusions

The seigneurial civilization of the Americas is among the least understood and is yet the most interesting in history. Two main obstacles have hindered a correct understanding of it. First, our tendency to sectional studies, thus neglecting the area whole, ranging from Canada to Argentina, and in regard to planter civilization, from the Mason-Dixon Line to Río de la Plata. The second, and worse, is the habit of applying to *homines and mores* of such civilizations our own yardstick, which is that of a bourgeois, urban, industrial, liberal-minded civilization.

The discovery and colonization of America was mainly achieved under the impulse of a rising capitalism; it was the bourgeoisie which had built both Italian and Flemish city-states and had given the impetus to Genoese and Venetian expansion all around the Mediterranean sea; it did the same later with Italian, Portuguese, Spanish, French, Dutch, and English expansion across the Atlantic. But when discovery and conquest occurred, the bourgeois class was not yet in power in any of the major nation-states of Europe. Everywhere it had to compromise with powers that were of pure medieval origin: absolute monarchy, universal church, military nobility. It was, there-

145

fore, a blend of such forces that built America. Monarchies, churches (both the Catholic and the English High Church, which was in the main, as Marx correctly observed, "a kind of Catholicism, putting the King on the Chair of the Pope"), and noblemen gave their military-political-ideological stamp to new transoceanic empires and colonies. The bourgeoisie wielded economic power, always trying to make the other groups operate in its interest and achieving in the main a tremendous success in "primary accumulation." From this operation, three hundred years later, the industrial revolution would find its capital for investment.

Even if themselves rapacious, desirous of glory and power, bellicose, intolerant, even sometimes bloodthirsty, the members of semi-feudal institutions tried, in many cases, to control the rapacity of capitalism, which by far overshadowed theirs; consequently, in the Spanish-American empire, the church, together with the monarchy, tried to protect the local peoples from the voracity of merchants and *conquistadores*. In New France, where the fur trade was being pushed to the last extremity by merchants, both Jesuit fathers and governors tried to limit it to some extent to protect the Indian nations.

It very soon appeared clear all over America which group was the most powerful. The capitalist world market was beginning to dictate its laws to the whole world, and colonial empires were attracted quickly into the whirlpool of this market. In French Canada, the monarchy, missionaries, and the rising seigneurial class were trying to build an unusual, utopian empire founded upon the Indian nations; and they, thanks to such extraordinary men as Champlain, would have succeeded, had it not been for the fur trade. International capitalist markets wanted furs; and New France had to sell them in order to survive and to be solvent. However, fur trade was the bone of contention among Canadian Indian nations, and so it was that the plan of the generous and remarkable Champlain crashed against the stumbling block of Iroquois hostility. New France needed the allegiance of the Indian nations, but it needed the fur trade more, since the colony (and this is the point), although governed by a seigneurial class, was dependent on international capitalist markets.

It was the same all over America. The large colonial empires, although discovered, conquered, and governed mainly by men from old-fashioned classes, had been built under the impulse of bourgeois economic expansion and to suit the needs of capitalism. Dependent on the capitalist world market, wholly subdued by its laws and will, colonial America harvested furs, tobacco, rice, sugar, cotton, coffee, and cocoa to supply the needs of international markets and imported slaves who were the "cheap money" by which mercantile capitalism paid for colonial raw products.

However, history is always "far more shrewd than men believe it to be," and it is exceedingly rare that things go as men plan them to go. Certainly mankind usually goes ahead following only its egotistic greeds and narrow-minded thirst for wealth and power; and consequently, men are always tricked by history. *Videbis, fili mi, quam parva sapientia regitur Mundus* ("You shall see, my son, how little wisdom is in the men who rule this world").* Indeed, Europe was exporting to the New World not only its merchants, its priests, its conquistadores—and its scum; the conquest was accomplished under both ideological and psychological impetus from a tremendous power drive. It was a whole culture, or, better, a complicated complex of cultures that crossed the ocean. The ideological cement that held the splendid fabric of American colonial empires together was the culture of the Italian Renaissance. It was an aristocratic, humanistic, classic culture; its *beau idéal* was the individual man of gentle blood, wide learning, outstanding courage. Leon Battista Alberti, Lodovico Ariosto, Baldassare Castiglione, Samuel de Champlain, Sir Walter Ralegh, even Hernán Cortés, personified in different ways such an ideal "Renaissance man." He was cruel and magnificent, gen-

---

* This quotation is attributed to Swedish Chancellor Axel Oxenstierna, who is said to have so informed his son John, when sending him to the European peace conference of Westphalia, 1648.

erous, authoritarian, paternalist, cultivated, open-minded, the very negation of democratic individualism, as he had only hatred and scorn for the *profanum vulgus;* always on the lookout for gold; however, only to spend it, even to waste it, never to invest it.

Consequently, undetected by capitalism, a singularly new civilization was rising in the Americas. The immediate, legitimate son of these Renaissance conquerors was the French-Canadian *gentilhomme,* as well as the southern and West-Indian planter, the Brazilian *senhor de engenho,* the Spanish-American *haciendado.* Certainly, the capitalist world market economically dominated these colonial empires; however, a class was rising to power in the New World that would confront the bourgeoisie, and compel it, in many cases, to a bloody fight for power.

Slavery, transplanted to the New World by capitalism as a ready-made tool for putting immense stretches of land to cultivation, with its precapitalist labor arrangement (it seems necessary to stress once again that where there is no wage labor, there is no capitalism), powerfully fostered the rise of the seigneurial class. Slavery developed the seigneurial habit of exercising a paternal yet absolute power, made of the seigneur not only an entrepreneur like the bourgeois industrialist, but also—and more—an absolute master, very like the feudal lord of the Middle Ages. Slavery created and fostered the patriarchal family, wholly different from the bourgeois family we are acquainted with; made of the seigneur a person who preferred to reveal his wealth, culture, and magnificent life, rather than to conceal money under plain clothes as the bourgeois did. It gave him, as an ideal, not profit (which, however energetically seigneurs sought it, was a means, not an end in itself), but status, political power, military service, and glory, so that the seigneur considered bearing arms and serving the state natural rights, to be exercised with moderation and statesmanship, almost like hereditary kings. Slavery impoverished the internal market and thus forestalled the industrial revolution, which can be based only upon mass production to cover a continuously increasing and highly dynamic market. It even allowed the seigneur to create an old-fashioned industry, wholly dependent on agriculture, in order to provide for immediate needs, and built—in the very center of the modern world—the last civilization in which country dominated over town.

Nowhere did this peculiar kind of seigneurial civilization achieve such a high development as in the United States and Brazil; but it was the Old South that soon fell into conflict with bourgeois, capitalist America, generated by Calvinist Dutch and Puritan New Englanders. In the beginning, the centers of capitalist power in the Americas were very small and limited, but the tremendous driving force of capitalism spelled doom for the old-fashioned seigneurial civilizations from the very start of the struggle.

However, the more the pressure grew on the Old South, the more self-conscious it became; the harder it tried to save its particular way of life and scale of values, the more it committed itself to the crucial experiment of trying to build its own "ideal state," wholly separated, based for the first time upon a seigneurial agrarian civilization *per se*. It was clear from the very beginning that it would mean war. War is really, for any kind of society, the "moment of truth." The war would measure the South's ability to accept the huge industrial conflict that the capitalist civilization was now able to wage.

Mercantile capitalism had coexisted reasonably well with seigneurial civilization (although the Canadian seigneurial society was swept away by the joint efforts of bourgeois New and Old England). As frequently observed, the growth of mercantilism in many cases was followed by an extension of slavery, and capitalist merchants made handsome profits in the slave trade. Newport, Rhode Island, for example, ". . . has been, in a great measure, built upon the blood of the poor Africans. . . ." [1] even if the bringing of thousands of slaves into America often met with stubborn resistance from seigneurial slave owners.

After the industrial revolution, capitalism began everywhere to overthrow the old-fashioned agrarian civilizations. It needed open markets, masses of "free" laborers, and an agrarian society to pay the expenses of industrialization. In other words, it needed contemporary colonialism. The industrial revolution, which prompted such expansionism, had even given tremendous destructive weapons to the modern, industrial nations; it had made possible the mobilization of millions of men and armed them with new, terrible engines of destruction on a heretofore unseen scale.

The South chose to accept battle on northern terms, the only choice it had, not only to resist aggression, but also to establish its own state founded on its own *Weltanschauung*. This seems to be the stumbling block for many historians who, unable to see the real essence of seigneurial civilization, insist on the South's being "capitalist." Capital usually moves toward the investment that looks more lucrative. Why did southern "capitalism" not rush into industrial production, thus making the South equal to the North in military terms, considering that war usually provides enormous profits? The fact was that southern "capital" (or better, southern money, which is far different) was mainly invested in slaves. To whom should southern slaveholders have sold their slaves in order to retrieve their money and so invest it in industrial production? This thought should suffice to show that southern civilization was not capitalist, as one of the basic characteristics of capitalism is high mobility of capital; however, this is not the point. The fact was that Confederate rulers did not want a private capitalist industry; they did not want to see a powerful industrial bourgeoisie rising in the Confederacy. Instead, they chose the way of "state socialism," a solution that is as far from capitalism as the earth is from the moon.

As for black slaves, if they, as it has been alleged, were accustomed to working as efficiently as modern workers on assemby lines, why were they not sent to "assemble" cannon, ironclads, submarines, locomotives, railroad cars? Why had the South to fight so painfully against a shortage of manpower? Assemblying, after all, does not require much skill, only automatic work, as Charlie Chaplin showed so well in *Modern Times*. The fact was that slavery was tied down to plantations; plantations were not "plants," but living units, not to be reckoned in purely economic terms, but more in social, human, psychological values. At any rate, this is another indication that plantation economy was not capitalist, as mobility of labor is another requisite of capitalism.[2] But, let us put aside such discussions. The Confederacy chose "state socialism." It organized it successfully and on a grandiose scale. What were, or, better, what might have been the consequences?

The Confederacy could not bring its unbelievable experiment to an end. It was defeated; it had to be defeated. For an old-fashioned agrarian community, it is utterly impossible to face modern technological warfare without being defeated. One has only to remember that against the twenty-eight ironclads built by the Confederacy, the Union not only built fifty-three, but even, at the same time, succeeded in selling ironclads abroad —the two big ironclad-steam-frigates *Re d'Italia* and *Re di Portogallo* of the Italian Royal Navy, which fought during the war of 1866, had been built in New York in 1862. This fact, far more than a million books and a billion statistics, helps to explain why the South lost the Civil War.[3]

However, this is not even the problem. To resist the tremendous onslaught of the foe, and to meet the needs of industrial warfare, the Confederacy had but one choice: "state socialism." It is amazing to see how clear-mindedly, how creatively southern leaders discovered this direction, previously unknown, and followed it. The man who, more than any other, embodied this stroke of genius was President Jefferson Davis. Be it only for this, he should rank among the major statesmen in history. His intelligence, his iron will, his capability in facing and solving such appalling problems were indeed amazing.

Certainly, Davis could not have foreseen the consequences that such a socioeconomic solution would most likely have brought with it. The South was defeated when its statist solution to economic problems was still in its "heroic age." In rejecting capitalism, obviously, the only way to industrialize is socialism. Certainly, it is amazing how the Confederacy managed to build up a tremendous war economy without allowing a capitalist class to rise. In a sense, its industry, from the most sophisticated, torpedo-making, to the greatest, the Augusta Powder Works, was still an old-fashioned, agrarian kind of industry, frequently relying upon makeshift, more worth the job of a *bricoleur* in the Levi-Strauss sense.

But what, then, had the Confederacy survived? Confederate leaders did their best to respect the basic characteristics of old agricultural societies (i.e., states' rights); and, in a sense, it is impressive to see how much they succeeded. It has even been argued that the Confederacy died of too much states' rights. However, from another viewpoint, Confederate "state socialism" was already beginning to display some of the most unsavory features of any statist economy: economic centralism, a ruthless intrusion into private property rights, and the rise of an embryonic military-economic bureaucracy. It is hard to see how, had the Confederacy survived the war, it could have been spared from wholesale economic planning, more and more centralism, bureaucracy, and finally complete take-over of all economic activity (indeed, of the national economy as a whole) by the government. Or were Confederate leaders thinking, perhaps, of giving up their national industry to private capitalists at the end of the war? It would have been national suicide; and history gives no example of any such hara-kiri by any ruling class.

Of course, such questions can have no answer; perhaps, they cannot even be asked. One might though surmise that the strong opposition to Confederate economic policy from such men as Governor Vance of North Carolina and even old Governor Brown of Georgia was prompted not only by egotism and wrongheadedness, but also in part (why not?) by a burgeoning distrust of a Confederacy that was risking the possibility of becoming a kind of Moloch socialist state.

Assuredly, history made by ifs is not only absurd, it may even be to no purpose, even ridiculous; so, let us stick to what really happened, putting aside the "might-have-beens." What happened was, in itself, amazing and almost incredible. If, as has been maintained, the meaning of life, both to individuals and to nations, is summarized and symbolized by the way they choose to die, one may conclude that the seigneurial class of the Old South (and of the Americas) is, indeed, a subject worth studying and understanding.

Notes

[1] Plato, *Timaeus*, 25, c,d. L. Annaeus Seneca, *Medea*, II, chorus.

[2] The first trip westward was made by the Genoese brothers Ugolino and Vadino Vivaldi (1291); the other Italians who followed, aboard (as captains) Portuguese and Spanish ships were: Antoniotto Usodimare, Lanzarotto Malocello, Da Noli and Da Recco, down to Colombo, Verrazzano, and Giovanni Caboto. (See Pierre Chaunu, *L'Expansion Européenne du XIII au XV Siècle*, Paris, 1969.)

[3] *Il Cortegiano*, by Baldassare Castiglione, was completed in a few days in 1508 (as the author himself states). At the end of the original manuscript (which is in Florence, Biblioteca Laureanziana), it is still possible to read the date "May 23, 1524." The first printing was in 1528, by the famous publisher Aldo Manuzio in Venice. Among the better contemporary editions is that edited by Vittorio Cian, Florence, 1894. The famous debate about "the true Courtesan" was placed by the author in the fascinating, almost magic Ducal Palace of Urbino; the "Sala delle Veglie" is still in pristine condition.

[4] Petrus Martyr ab Angleria, *Decades de Orbe Novo*, 1, 2, 53.

[5] *Scritti di Cristoforo Colombo Pubblicati e Illustrati da Cesare de Lollis*, Vol. 1, Rome, 1894, p. 120 ff.

[6] Lawrence C. Wroth, *The Voyages of Giovanni da Verrazzano, 1524–1528*, New Haven, Conn., 1972, with complete reproduction and translation of writings.

[7] W. F. Craven, *The Southern Colonies in the Seventeenth Century*, Baton Rouge, La., 1949; J. T. Lanning, *The Spanish Missions of Georgia*, Chapel Hill, N.C., 1935.

[8] W. Notenstein, *The English People on the Eve of Colonization*, New York, 1962, p. 112.

[9] *Ibid.*, p. 26.

[10] The life of Richard Eden is obscure; he seems to have been born in Herefordshire, England, in 1521. (See E. Arber, *The First Three Books on America*, several editions.)

[11] Richard Willes taught rhetoric in Perugia until 1572; his work was printed in London in 1577 and dedicated to the Countess of Bedford.

[12] Information about and a bibliography of Ramusio are to be found in G. B. Parks, "Ramusio's Literary History," *Studies in Philology*, Vol. LII (1955), p. 127 ff. The best biography is still A. Del Piero's "Della vita e degli studi di Gio. Battista Ramusio" in "Nuovo Archivio Veneto", n.s., Vol. IV, 1902, p. 5 ff.

[13] F. M. Rogers, "Hakluyt as Translator" in *Hakluyt Handbook*, Vol. 1, D. B. Quinn, ed., London, 1974, p. 37 ff.

[14] *Ibid.*, quot., p. 43.

[15] G. B. Parks, "Tudor Travel Literature: A Brief History" in *Hakluyt Handbook*, *ibid.*, quot., p. 105.

[16] D. B. Quinn, *Ralegh and the British Empire*, London, 1947.

CHAPTER 2—RALEGH, THE RENAISSANCE HERO

[1] Pierre Lefranc, *Sir Walter Ralegh écrivain: l'oeuvre et les idées*, Paris, 1968, p. 614 ff. Unluckily, such distinguished authors as Mario Praz, Vincent Luciani, E. A. Strathmann, and F. Raab, in order to establish the cultural link between R. and Machiavelli, have relied mainly on such works as *The Cabinet Council* and *The Maxims of State*, which more recent scholarship has demonstrated to be spurious. Only Pierre Lefranc, quot., has established in a satisfactory way the decisive influence of Machiavelli upon Ralegh's thought.

[2] *Ibid.*

[3] Agnes Latham, ed., *The Poems of Sir Walter Ralegh*, Cambridge, Mass., 1962, pp. 13–18, 44.

[4] *Ibid.*, quot., p. xiii.

[5] M. Fishwick, *Gentlemen of Virginia*, New York, 1961, p. 10.

[6] Latham, *op. cit.*, quot., p. 27.

[7] Lefranc, *op. cit.*, quot.

[8] Giambattista Vico, *La Scienza Nuova Seconda*, a cura di F. Nicolini, Bari, Italy, 1953, p. 22.

[9] "Discourse of Westerne Planting by Richard Hakluyt, 1584," in *The Original Writings and Correspondence of the Two Richard Hakluyts*, Vol. 2, E. G. R. Taylor, ed., London, 1935, p. 211 ff.
[10] Jacob Burckhardt, *La Civiltà del Rinascimento in Italia*, Firenze, Italy, 1943, p. 160.
[11] W. Oakeshott, *The Queen and the Poet*, London, 1960, p. 154. This book, although declared by Pierre Lefranc to be *"fantaisiste en matière de dates, d'attribution et d'interprétation,"* gives several verses by Ralegh not found in the *Poems* edited by Agnes Latham.
[12] Latham, *op. cit.*, quot., p. 44.
[13] *Ibid.*, quot., p. 28.

CHAPTER 3—THE IDEOLOGICAL BASIS FOR SECTIONAL CULTURES

[1] E. D. Genovese, *The World the Slaveholders Made*, New York, 1969, p. 12.
[2] A. Weber, *Storia della Filosofia Europea*, Vol. 2, Milan, Italy, 1929, p. 25.
[3] The discovery was made by Professor Gonnet, now of the University of Upsala, Sweden, who communicated his finding to me personally.
[4] Richard Beale Davis, *Literature and Society in Early Virginia*, Baton Rouge, La., 1973, p. xvi.
[5] It was certainly true that Galileo had to print his last great book in Calvinist Holland. Calvinist civilization was always more liberal toward scientific culture (even if Calvin burned Servetus to death while he was working on his discovery of the circulation of blood). However, classicism, supposed to be heathen and Catholic, was at the same time usually forbidden, or paid only lip service.
[6] Howard Mumford Jones, *O Strange New World—American Culture: the Formative Years*, New York, 1952, p. 107.

CHAPTER 4—NEW FRANCE, CORNERSTONE OF THE
SEIGNEURIAL SOCIETY

[1] I have no intention of rediscussing the problem of "cliometrics" and slavery; it will suffice to refer the reader to the penetrating study by H. G. Gutman, "The World Two Cliometricians Made," first printed in *The Journal of Negro History*, Vol. LX, No. 1 (January 1975), p. 53 ff.; and the conference "Time on the Cross: A First Appraisal," University of Rochester, 1974, under the chairmanship of Professor R. Rosett, in which the writer had the honor of participating.

² The contention that slave societies were capitalist has been cogently refuted by E. D. Genovese in his works.

³ E. Donnan, ed., *Documents Illustrative of the History of the Slave Trade to America*, 4 vols., Washington, D.C., 1930 ff.

⁴ *Ibid.*, Vol. 4, quot., p. 131 ff.

⁵ E. Foner, "Redefining the Past" in *Labor History*, Vol. 16, No. 1 (Winter 1975), p. 127 ff.

⁶ W. J. Eccles, *France in America*, New York, 1972, p. 122.

⁷ E. D. Genovese, *The Political Economy of Slavery*, New York, 1966, p. 283.

⁸ M. Trudel, *L'Esclavage au Canada Français*, Québec, 1960.

⁹ M. Trudel, *Les Débuts du Régime Seigneurial au Canada*, Montréal, Canada, 1974.

¹⁰ Eccles, *op. cit.*, quot., p. 113.

¹¹ *Ibid.*, quot., p. 114.

¹² P. H. Wood, *Black Majority*, New York, 1974.

¹³ W. J. Eccles, *The Canadian Frontier, 1534–1760*, Albuquerque, N.M., 1969, p. 89.

CHAPTER 5—THE "TROPICAL CIVILIZATION"

¹ A. E. Smith, *Colonists in Bondage: White Servitude and Convict Labor in America, 1607–1776*, Chapel Hill, N.C., 1947.

² P. H. Wood, *Black Majority*, New York, 1974, quot., *passim*.

³ R. H. Pearce, *Savagism and Civilization*, Baltimore, Md., 1953.

⁴ G. Freyre, *New World in the Tropics*, New York, 1945, p. 154 ff.

⁵ J. R. Mandle, "The Plantation Economy: an Essay in Definition" in *The Slave Economies*, Vol. 1, E. D. Genovese, ed., New York, 1973, p. 214 ff.

⁶ *Ibid.*, quot., p. 225.

⁷ R. B. Sheridan, *Sugar and Slavery—An Economic History of the British West Indies, 1623–1775*, Baltimore, Md., 1973, p. 18 ff.

⁸ E. Donnan, ed., *Documents Illustrative of the History of the Slave Trade to America*, 4 vols., Washington, D.C., 1930, Vol. 4, quote.

⁹ On the seigneurial class of the British West Indies, see Sheridan, *op. cit.*, quot.; R. S. Dunn, *Sugar and Slaves—The Rise of the Planter Class in the English West Indies, 1624–1713*, New York, 1972; O. Patterson, *The Sociology of Slavery—An Analysis of the Origins, Development and Structure of Negro Slave Society in Jamaica*, Cranbury, N.J., 1969; C. and L. Bridenbaugh, *No Peace Beyond the Line—The English in the Caribbean, 1624–1690*, New

York, 1972. On the French West Indies: A. Gisler, *L'Esclavage aux Antilles Françaises*, Fribourg, Switzerland, 1965; Gaston-Martin, *L'Esclavage dans les Colonies Françaises*, Paris, 1948.

[10] Dunn, *ibid.*, quot., p. 296 ff.

[11] *Ibid.*, quot., p. 116.

[12] *Ibid.*, quot., p. 264.

[13] *Ibid.*, quot., p. 279.

[14] W. J. Eccles, *France in America*, New York, 1972, quot., p. 148 ff.

[15] E. D. Genovese, *The World the Slaveholders Made*, New York, 1969, quot., p. viii.

[16] G. Freyre, *Casa Grande e Senzala—Formaçâo da Familia Brasileira sob o Regime de Economia Patriarcal*, Rio de Janeiro, 1958, p. 247.

[17] *Ibid.*, quot., p. 426 ff.

[18] *Ibid.*, quot.; English translation: *The Masters and the Slaves*, New York, 1970, p. xxv.

[19] *Ibid.*, quot., p. 430.

[20] *Ibid.*, quot., p. 240.

[21] Jones Family Papers, University of Georgia Library, Manuscripts Division, Athens, Ga. (partially printed by R. M. Myers, *The Children of Pride—A True Story of Georgia and the Civil War*, New Haven, Conn., and London, 1972).

[22] Freyre, *Casa Grande, op. cit.*, quot., p. 400 ff.

[23] E. Bradford Burns, *A History of Brazil*, New York, 1970, p. 194; L. Bethell, *The Abolition of the Brazilian Slave Trade*, Cambridge, England, 1970.

[24] D. T. Lawson, *No Heir to Take Its Place—The Story of Rice in Georgetown County, South Carolina*, published by the Rice Museum, Georgetown, S.C., 1972, p. 28.

[25] F. Tannenbaum, *Ten Keys to Latin America*, New York, 1960, p. 80.

[26] E. D. Genovese, *The Political Economy of Slavery*, New York, quot., *passim*.

[27] *Ibid.*, quot., p. 171.

[28] Freyre, *Casa Grande, op. cit.*, quot., p. 241.

[29] C. Vann Woodward, *American Counterpoint—Slavery and Racism in the North-South Dialogue*, Boston, Mass., 1964, p. 27.

[30] Freyre, *New World, op. cit.*, quot., p. 4.

[31] Freyre, *Casa Grande, op. cit.*, quot., p. 231.

[32] Elise Pinckney and others, eds., *The Letterbook of Eliza Lucas Pinckney, 1739–1762*, Chapel Hill, N.C., 1972, p. 9 f.

[33] *Ibid.*, Eliza Lucas Pinckney to Mrs. Boddicott, May 2, 1741, quot., p. 13 f.

[34] *Ibid.*, May 2, 1740, quot., p. 6 ff.

[35] *Ibid.*, Eliza Lucas Pinckney to Miss Bartlett, c. March-April 1742, quot., p. 32 f.

[36] W. B. Edgar, ed., *The Letterbook of Robert Pringle*, 2 vols. Columbia, S.C., 1972, Vol. I, p. xvi.

[37] Freyre, *Casa Grande, op. cit.*, quot., p. 378; C. R. Boxer, *Salvador de Sà and the Struggle for Brazil and Angola, 1602–1686,* Westport, Conn., 1975.

[38] E. D. Genovese, *Roll, Jordan, Roll—The World the Slaves Made*, New York, 1974.

[39] *Ibid.*; J. H. Johnston, *Race Relations in Virginia and Miscegenation in the South, 1776–1860*, Amherst, Mass., 1970.

CHAPTER 6—THE IMPACT OF THE INDUSTRIAL REVOLUTION

[1] H. D. Woodman, *King Cotton and His Retainers*, Lexington, Ky., 1968, p. 8.

[2] M. Dobb, *Studies in the Development of Capitalism*, New York, 1947.

[3] C. M. Cipolla, *La Rivoluzione Industriale*, Torino, Italy, 1975, p. 11.

[4] S. J. Stein, *Vassouras—A Brazilian Coffee-County, 1850–1890*, New York, 1970.

[5] R. Luraghi, "Problemi Economici dell'Italia Unita, 1861–1918" in *Nuove Questioni di Storia del Risorgimento e dell'Unità d'Italia*, Vol. 2, Milan, Italy, 1961, p. 389 ff.

[6] Mainly in Vol. 1.

[7] Woodman, *op. cit.*, quot.; T. P. Kettell, *Southern Wealth and Northern Profits*, F. M. Green, ed., University, Ala., 1965.

[8] E. Foner, *Free Soil, Free Labor, Free Men—The Ideology of the Republican Party Before the Civil War*, New York, 1970.

[9] R. Luraghi, *Storia della Guerra Civile Americana*, 4th ed., Torino, Italy, 1976.

CHAPTER 7—SOUTHERN CIVILIZATION AT ITS PEAK

[1] M. Fishwick, *Gentlemen of Virginia*, New York, 1961, quot., *passim*.

[2] W. R. Taylor, *Cavalier and Yankee, The Old South and American National Character*, Garden City, N.Y., 1963, p. 325, n. 32.

[3] E. A. Miles, "The Old South and the Classical World," *The North Carolina Historical Review*, Summer 1971, p. 258, n. 3, ff.

[4] *Ibid.*

[5] Allston Family Papers, Charles Allston to Robert F. W. Allston,

December 22, 1860, South Carolina Historical Society Library, Manuscript Collection, Charleston, S.C.

[6] *Ibid.* J. B. Allston to W. Allen Allston, several items.

[7] Howell Cobb Papers, Mary Ann Lamar to John Basil Lamar, January 18, 1835, University of Georgia Library, Manuscript Division, Athens, Ga.

[8] M. E. Rutherford, *The South in History and Literature*, Atlanta, Ga., 1907, p. 307.

[9] Howell Cobb Papers, John B. Lamar to Mary Ann Lamar, November 22, 1838, *op. cit.*

[10] Allston Family Papers, Adele Allston to Charles Allston, April 1862, *op. cit.*

[11] "Sketches of the South Santee" in *Travels in the Old South, Selected from Periodicals of the Times*, 2 vols., E. L. Schwab, ed., Lexington, Ky., 1973, Vol. 1, p. 3 ff.

[12] P. H. Wood, *Black Majority*, New York, 1974, quot., p. 110, n.

[13] G. Freyre, *Sobrados e Mucambos. Decadéncia do Patriarcado rural e desenvolvimento do urbano*, Rio de Janeiro, 1936, p. 181.

[14] See *The Letterbook of Robert Pringle*, quot.; and P. M. Hamer and others, eds., *The Papers of Henry Laurens*, Columbia, S.C., 1968 ff (4 volumes to date).

[15] E. D. Genovese, *The Political Economy of Slavery*, New York, 1972, quot., p. 210, n. 11.

[16] *Ibid.*, quot., p. 172.

[17] J. T. Lanning, *The Spanish Missions of Georgia*, Chapel Hill, N.C., 1935.

[18] F. Tannenbaum, *Slave and Citizen*, New York, 1947, p. 117 f.

[19] E. P. Skinner, ed., *Peoples and Cultures of Africa*, Garden City, N.Y., 1973.

[20] J. B. Christiense, "The Role of Proverbs in Fante Culture," *ibid.*, quot., p. 509 ff. N. E. Whitten, Jr., and J. F. Szwed, eds., *Afro-American Anthropology—Contemporary Perspectives*, New York, 1970.

[21] J. H. Kwabena Nketia, "African Music" in *Skinner, op. cit.*, quot., p. 580 ff.; J. F. Szwed, "Afro-American Musical Adaptation" in Whitten and Szwed, *ibid.*, quot., p. 219 ff.

[22] E. E. Thorpe, *The Old South: a Psychohistory*, Durham, N.C., 1972. J. Kovel, *White Racism: A Psychohistory*, New York, 1970.

[23] Howell Cobb Papers, J. B. Lamar to Sister, January 27, 1835, *op. cit.*

[24] Charles Francis Adams, Jr., to his father, November 2, 1864, in *A Cycle of Adams Letters*, Vol. II, p. 215.

[25] In *Civil War History*, Vol. 19, n. 3 (September 1973), p. 280 ff.

[26] R. E. May, *The Southern Dream of a Caribbean Empire*, Baton Rouge, La., 1973.

[27] E. J. Warner, *Generals in Gray*, Baton Rouge, La., 1959.

[28] Howell Cobb Papers, John B. Lamar to Sister, January 27, 1835, *op. cit.*

[29] Cobb-Erwin-Lamar Collection, J. B. Lamar to Howell Cobb, October 26, 1842, University of Georgia Library, Manuscript Division, Athens, Ga.

[30] *Ibid.*, J. B. Lamar to Sister, May 23, 1846.

[31] A satisfying biography of Jefferson Davis is still to be written.

[32] See my essay "The Civil War and the Modernization of American Society," *Civil War History*, September 1972.

[33] Antonio Gramsci, *Gli Intellettuali e l'Organizzazione della Cultura*, Torino, Italy, 1958.

[34] Georg Weber, *Storia Universale*, Vol. 2, Milan, Italy, 1881, p. 434.

[35] A. R. Writh to Mr. (?) Cobb, December 19, 1841. Private collection.

[36] Howell Cobb Papers, J. B. Lamar to Sister, November 7, 1838, *op. cit.*

[37] *Ibid.*, J. B. Lamar to Howell Cobb, January 3, 1849.

[38] C. Eaton, *The Growth of Southern Civilization*, New York, 1961, p. 196.

CHAPTER 8—THE OLD SOUTH AND THE NEW INDUSTRIAL WARFARE

[1] R. Luraghi, "The Civil War and the Modernization of American Society," *Civil War History*, September 1972.

[2] J. F. C. Fuller, *The Conduct of War*, London, 1962.

[3] Niccolò Machiavelli, *Dell'Arte della Guerra*, Firenze, Italy, 1521.

[4] A. Toynbee, *A Study of History*, Vol. 4, London, 1939, p. 151.

[5] C. Cipolla, "La rivoluzione industriale" in *Storia delle idee politiche, economiche e sociali*, Vol. 5, Torino, Italy, 1972, p. 11 ff.

[6] Edward M. Earle, ed., *Makers of Modern Strategy—Military Thought from Machiavelli to Hitler*, New York, 1966, p. 151.

CHAPTER 9—THE FEEBLENESS OF THE SOUTHERN WAR ECONOMY

[1] R. Luraghi, *Storia della Guerra Civile Americana*, 4th ed., Torino, Italy, quot., p. 132 ff.; P. Pieri, "Carlo Bianco, conte di Saint-Jorioz e il suo Trattato sulla guerra partigiana" in *Bollettino Storico-Bibliografico Subalpino*, Vol. LV, No. 2 (1957) and Vol.

LVI, No. 1 (1958); E. Liberti, ed., *Tecniche della guerra partigiana nel Risorgimento*, Firenze, Italy, 1972.

[2] R. Luraghi, "The Civil War and the Modernization of American Society," *Civil War History*, September 1972. *Guerra Civile Americana, op. cit.*, quot., p. 127 ff.

[3] Military studies on such wars are scarce, if available at all.

[4] Antonio Gramsci, *Gli Intellettuali e L'Organizzazione della Cultura*, Torino, Italy, 1958, quot.

[5] E. D. Genovese, *The Political Economy of Slavery*, New York, 1972, quot., p. 158.

[6] *Ibid.*, quot., p. 161.

[7] C. B. Dew, *Ironmaker to the Confederacy—Joseph R. Anderson and the Tredegar Iron Works*, New Haven, Conn., and London, 1966; K. Bruce, *Virginia Iron Manufacture in the Slave Era*, New York, 1930.

[8] R. Luraghi, "Problemi Economici dell'Italia Unita, 1861–1918" in *Nuove Questioni di Storia del Risorgimento e dell'Unità d'Italia*, Vol. 2, Milan, Italy, 1961, quot.

[9] G. D'Annunzio, *Laudi del Cielo, della Terra, del Mare e degli Eroi*, Vol. 4, "*Merope,*" Vittoriale, 1939, p. 112.

[10] Genovese, *op. cit.*, quot., p. 160.

[11] E. Armes, *The Story of Coal and Iron in Alabama*, Birmingham, Ala., 1910, p. 61 ff.

[12] Bruce, *op. cit.*, quot., p. 276.

[13] W. N. Still, Jr., *Confederate Shipbuilding*, Athens, Ga., 1969, *passim.*

[14] E. Merto Coulter, *The Confederate States of America*, Baton Rouge, La., 1950, p. 202.

[15] Still, *op. cit.*, quot., p. 44.

[16] R. D. Goff, *Confederate Supply*, Durham, N.C., 1969, p. 4.

[17] *Ibid.*, quot., p. 4.

CHAPTER 10—FORCED INDUSTRIALIZATION THROUGH STATE SOCIALISM

[1] Barrington Moore, Jr., *Social Origins of Dictatorship and Democracy, Lord and Peasant in the Making of the Modern World*, Boston, Mass., 1966, p. 41 f.

[2] M. Dobb, *Soviet Economic Development Since 1917*, special Italian edition revised by the author as *Storia dell'Economia Sovietica*, Rome, 1957, p. 226.

[3] *Ibid.*, quot., p. 231.

[4] W. Churchill, *The Second World War*, Part 4, Vol. 2, London, 1951, p. 108.

[5] S. N. Prokopovic, *Histoire économique de l'URSS*, Paris, 1952, p. 303.

[6] G. Stalin, *Questioni del Leninismo*, Moscow, 1946, p. 401 ff.

[7] *Ibid.*

[8] M. Djilas, *La Nouvelle Classe*, Paris, 1955. Leon Trotsky, *La Révolution trahie*, Paris, 1936.

[9] D. Rowland, ed., *Jefferson Davis, Constitutionalist: His Letters, Papers and Speeches*, 10 vols., Jackson, Miss., 1923, Vol. 5, p. 216 f.

[10] R. C. Todd, *Confederate Finance*, Athens, Ga., 1954, p. 25.

[11] E. Capers, *The Life and Times of Christopher G. Memminger*, Richmond, Va., 1893, p. 342.

[12] Todd, *op. cit.*, quot., p. 34 f.

[13] The basic documents of such loans are to be found in *The Journal of the Congress of the Confederate States of America*, 7 vols., Washington, D.C., 1904.

[14] James H. Hammond Papers, H. V. Johnson to James H. Hammond, August 29, 1861, Library of Congress, Manuscript Division, Washington, D.C.

[15] Todd, *op. cit.*, quot. p. 82 ff.

[16] J. C. Schwab, *The Confederate States of America, 1861–1865: A Financial and Industrial Story of the South During the Civil War*, New York, 1901, p. 43.

[17] R. Luraghi, *Storia della Guerra Civile Americana*, 4th ed., Torino, Italy, 1976, quot., p. 1279 ff.

[18] Todd, *op. cit.*, quot., p. 140 f.

[19] C. G. Memminger Papers, Jefferson Davis Papers, Duke University Library, Manuscript Collection, Chapel Hill, N.C.

[20] R. Andreano, ed., *The Economic Impact of the American Civil War*, Cambridge, Mass., 1962, tables.

[21] *Ibid.*, quot., pp. 76, 171 ff.

[22] I. Unger, *The Greenback Era*, Princeton, N.J., 1964; R. P. Sharkey, *Money Class and Party—An Economic Study of Civil War and Reconstruction*, Baltimore, Md., 1959.

[23] It has been debated for a long time whether Secretary Floyd had treacherously sent weapons to southern arsenals on the eve of secession; now, studies by Meriwether Stuart (who wrote several articles on the subject in *The Virginia Magazine of History and Biography*) have conclusively demonstrated that he did; the weapons, however, were like a drop in the ocean.

[24] Tredegar Company Papers, Letter books, J. R. Anderson to J. A. Seddon, December 1862, Virginia State Library and Archives, Richmond, Va.

[25] E. M. Coulter, *The Confederate States of America*, Baton Rouge, La., 1950, quot., p. 203; C. W. Ramsdell, *Behind the Lines in the Southern Confederacy*, Baton Rouge, La., 1944, and "The

Confederate Government and the Railroads" in *The American Historical Review*, 1917, p. 22; M. E. Massey, *Ersatz in the Confederacy*, Columbia, S.C., 1952.

[26] *Ibid.*, Massey, quot., p. 39.

[27] *Ibid.*

[28] Emory M. Thomas, *The Confederacy as a Revolutionary Experience*, Englewood Cliffs, N.J., 1971, p. 89. National Archives, Washington, D.C., Record Groups 56, 68 (hereafter RG), Contracts, esp. 18, 27, 28.

[29] Tredegar Company Papers, S. R. Mallory to J. R. Anderson, July 24, 1861, *op. cit.*

[30] J. P. Lesley, *Iron Manufacturer's Guide*, Philadelphia, Pa., 1859, p. 224 ff.

[31] F. Vandiver, *Ploughshares into Swords: Josiah Gorgas and Confederate Ordnance*, Austin, Texas, 1951, p. 62 f.

[32] Shelby Iron Company Papers, Colin J. McRae to Albert Jones, November 5, 1862, University of Alabama Library, Tuscaloosa, Ala. National Archives. RG 56, 68, Contracts. quot.

[33] K. Coleman, *Confederate Athens*, Athens, Ga., 1967.

[34] Coulter, *op. cit.*, quot., p. 275; R. C. Blach, III, *The Railroads of the Confederacy*, Chapel Hill, N.C., 1952; G. E. Turner, *Victory Rode the Rails*, Indianapolis and New York, 1953.

[35] *Ibid.*, Coulter, quot., p. 280 f.

[36] *Ibid.*, quot., p. 204.

[37] *The War of the Rebellion—Official Records of the Union and Confederate Armies* (hereafter, OR), Series IV, Vol. 1, p. 618 ff.

[38] Coulter, *op. cit.*, quot., p. 208; Massey, *op. cit.*, quot., p. 161.

[39] Adjutant General's Correspondence, Mallet's Memorandum, 1862, National Archives, Washington, D.C., RG 109.

[40] W. G. Rains, *History of the Confederate Powder Works*, Augusta, Ga., 1882.

[41] F. Vandiver, ed., *The Civil War Diary of General Josiah Gorgas*, University, Ala., 1947, p. 90.

[42] Coulter, *op. cit.*, quot., p. 206.

[43] Vandiver, *op. cit.*, quot.

[44] *U.S. Census*, 1860.

[45] W. N. Still, Jr., *Confederate Shipbuilding*, Athens, Ga., 1969, quot., *passim*.

[46] *Ibid.*, quot., p. 33.

[47] Minutes of the City Council, Public Library, Columbus, Ga.

[48] Records of the Naval Gun Foundry and Ordnance Works, Letter books (4 vols.), National Archives, Washington, D.C., RG 45; Colin J. McRae Papers, Alabama State Department of Archives and History, Montgomery, Ala.

[49] Still, *op. cit.*, quot., p. 86 and n. 25.

[50] *Ibid.*, quot., p. 80.

[51] W. N. Still, Jr., *Iron Afloat—The Story of Confederate Armorclads*, Nashville, Tenn., 1971, p. 227.

[52] OR, Series I, Vol. XXIII, Part 2, p. 773 ff.

[53] Coulter, *op. cit.*, quot., p. 210; C. W. Ramsdell, "The Control of Manufacturing by the Confederate Government," *The Mississippi Valley Historical Review*, Vol. 8 (1921), p. 245.

[54] F. C. Corley, *Confederate City: Augusta, Georgia, During the Civil War*, Augusta, Ga., 1970.

[55] *Ibid.*, quot., p. 49.

[56] D. W. Standard, *Columbus, Georgia, in the Confederacy*, New York, 1954.

[57] E. Armes, *The Story of Coal and Iron in Alabama*, Birmingham, Ala., 1910, quot., p. 135.

[58] Still, *Confederate Shipbuilding, op. cit.*, quot., p. 55.

[59] Tredegar Company Papers, J. R. Anderson to Secretaries of War and Navy, December 9, 1864, and several other letters of the time, mainly to General Josiah Gorgas and Commander John M. Brooke, Virginia State Library and Archives, Richmond, Va.

CHAPTER 11—TRANSPORTATION AND THE
NATIONALIZATION OF FOREIGN TRADE

[1] E. M. Coulter, *The Confederate States of America*, Baton Rouge, La., 1950, quot., p. 270 ff.

[2] L. B. Hill, "State Socialism in the Confederate States of America," *Southern Sketches*, First Series, No. 9, Charlottesville, Va., 1936.

[3] Coulter, *op. cit.*, quot., p. 288 f.

[4] James D. Bulloch, *The Secret Service of the Confederate States in Europe: or, How the Confederate Cruisers Were Equipped*, 2 vols., New York, 1959.

[5] Coulter, *op. cit.*, quot., p. 291.

[6] Governor Vance Letter books, North Carolina Department of Archives and History, Raleigh, N.C.

[7] Bulloch, *op. cit.*, Vol. 2, quot., p. 225 f.

[8] OR, Series IV, Vol. III, pp. 28, 554; Vol. II, p. 1013 f.

[9] C. S. Davis, *Colin J. McRae, Confederate Financial Agent*, Tuscaloosa, Ala., 1961.

[10] OR, Series IV, Vol. III, pp. 78 ff, 80 ff.

[11] Hill, *op. cit.*, quot., p. 14.

[12] *Ibid.*, quot., p. 15.

[13] *Official Records of the Union and Confederate Navies in the War of the Rebellion* (hereafter, ORN), Series II, Vol. II, p. 224.

[14] F. L. Owsley, *States Rights in the Confederacy*, Chicago, Ill., 1925.

[15] R. H. Crallé, ed., *The Works of John Calhoun*, 6 vols., New York, 1854 ff.; Papers of John Calhoun, Clemson University Library, Clemson, S.C.

CHAPTER 12—THE CLIMAX OF UTOPIA: CONFEDERATE EMANCIPATION

[1] M. E. Massey, *Ersatz in the Confederacy*, Columbia, S.C., 1952, quot., p. 27.

[2] R. Durden, *The Gray and the Black—The Confederate Debate on Emancipation*, Baton Rouge, La., 1972, p. 30 ff.

[3] OR, Series I, Vol. LII, Part 2, p. 586 ff.

[4] OR, Series IV, Vol. III, p. 1161 ff.

[5] Durden, *op. cit.*, quot., pp. 225 ff, 244, 273 ff.

[6] The best discussion of the true nature of the Emancipation Proclamation is to be found in J. G. Randall, *Constitutional Problems Under Lincoln*, Urbana, Ill., 1951.

[7] Durden, *op. cit.*, quot., pp. 48, 77, 102, 209, 272, 280.

CONCLUSIONS

[1] E. Donnan, ed., *Documents Illustrative of the History of the Slave Trade to America*, 4 vols., Washington, D.C., 1930, Vol. 4, quot., p. 68 ff., Dr. S. Hopkins to Mose Brown, April 29, 1784. The resistance of slaveholders to excessive slave trade is well illustrated by *ibid.*, Vol. 4, pp. 14 f, 23 f, 68 f, 122 ff, 127 f, 131 ff, 137 f, 140 ff, 151 f, 155 f, 158 ff, 161 ff.

[2] I remember Professor Fogel, at the end of the Rochester Conference, Fall 1974, admitting with remarkable intellectual fairness that slaves turned out to be "efficient" when working on cotton and "inefficient" when working on grain, indicating the correctness of the criticism that the high "profits" yielded by cotton were generated by an international trade-market conjuncture and not by a superiority of slave labor over free.

[3] Papers regarding the building of the *Re d'Italia*, Mariner Museum Library, Norfolk, Va.

Bibliography

The following is neither a complete list of primary and secondary sources consulted nor a full list of bibliographic material. It is intended simply as a guide for further reading and research. The sources given below are those which the author found most useful in the preparation of this book.

SOURCES

UNPUBLISHED MATERIAL

Italian Archives

Biblioteca Vaticana, Roma. Collezione Ottoboniana (includes several rare volumes pertaining to early America); Collezione Urbinate (material on early Virginia).

Archivio di Stato di Genova, Genova. Manoscritti della Sala Colombiana.

Archivio di Stato di Milano, Milano. Carteggio generale (includes letters re John Cabot).

Spanish Archives

Archivo General de Indias, Sevilla. Papeles de Estado; Papeles procedentes de Cuba, Florida y México; Sección quinta, Papeles de gobierno de las Secretarías de Despacho y Consejo de Indias;

Audiencia de Santo Domingo; Patronato; Indiferente General (esp. Legajo 2869).
Biblioteca Colombina, Sevilla. Books read and used by Columbus, with notes.
Archivo Histórico Nacional, Simancas. Papeles de Estado; several "Secciones."

French Archives
Archives Nationales, Paris. Colonies, Série A-G; Marine, Série B²-B⁷. (The most useful are series C, Colonies, on the different colonies, and series F, with the Colonial Codes).
Bibliothèque Nationale, Dépt. de Manuscrits, Paris. Fonds Français (much material on French West Indies and Louisiana); Mélanges de Colbert (a good deal on New France); Collection Clairambault.
Bibliothèque de l'Arsenal, Paris. Manuscripts (much on the economic life of Canada).
Archives du Ministère des Affaires Étrangères, Paris. Mémoires et Documents, Amérique.

British Archives
Public Records Office, London. State Papers, Domestic; Admiralty Letters; Colonial Office Papers, Class 5, America and West Indies; Plantations general (material re sugar production in the islands); Promiscuous and private letters (re internal life of the colonies: Virginia, Antigua, Bahamas, Barbadoes—esp. original correspondence with the Board of Trade); Treasury Papers, In and Out Letters; High Court of Admiralty Papers, Miscellaneous; Intercepted Letters; Foreign Office Papers.

Canadian Archives
Archives du Seminaire de Québec, Québec. Polygraphie.

United States Archives
National Archives, Washington, D.C. Record Group 109, War Department Collection of Confederate Records, letters sent and received by the Confederate Secretary of War; Correspondence of Adjutant and Inspector General; Quartermaster General's Office; Inspector General of field transportation; Railroad Bureau; Records of the Chief of Ordnance; Record Group 59, Intercepted letters from Confederate Ordnance Bureau in the Files of Union Department of State; Record Group 45, Naval Records Collection of the Office of Naval Records and Library, Office of Ordnance and Hydrography (however, several records pertaining to this office are to be found in Record Groups 37, 74, and

109); Records of the Selma Naval Gun Foundry and Ordnance Works (exceedingly important); Record Group 365, Treasury Department Collection of Confederate Records (very useful, though the contracts are mainly in Record Group 109).

Library of Congress, Manuscripts Division, Washington, D.C. James H. Hammond Papers; Catesby ap Jones Papers; Matthew F. Maury Papers.

University of Notre Dame Library, Notre Dame. William T. Sherman Papers.

Buffalo and Erie Historical Society Library, Buffalo. E. J. Warner Letterbook (Warner was Chief Engineer in the Confederate Navy).

New York Historical Society Library, New York. Gustavus V. Fox Papers (mostly unpublished; esp. his post-war correspondence with the Confederate gun-maker Catesby ap Jones).

Virginia Historical Society Library, Richmond. The Minor Family Papers; Robert E. Lee Papers.

Virginia State Archives, Richmond. Tredegar Iron Company Papers.

Confederate Memorial Literary Society, Richmond. Jefferson Davis Papers.

Norfolk Public Library, Norfolk. W. Whittle Papers.

Southern Historical Collection, University of North Carolina, Chapel Hill. Stephen R. Mallory Diary; Admiral Buchanan Letterbook.

Miami University Library, Oxford. Jefferson Davis Papers.

Duke University Library, Durham. Jefferson Davis Papers; Christopher G. Memminger Papers; James D. B. DeBow Papers; Stephen R. Mallory Papers; J. N. Maffitt Papers.

North Carolina Department of Archives and History, Raleigh. Zebulon B. Vance Papers; Governor's Letterbooks.

South Carolina Department of Archives, Columbia. Military Affair 1860–1865; Public Records of South Carolina.

South Caroliniana Library, Columbia. John C. Calhoun Papers; Allston Family Papers; Confederate Department of Engineers Papers.

South Carolina Historical Society Library, Charleston. Allston Family Collection; Pinckney Papers; Middleton Papers.

Charleston Library Society, Charleston. W. G. Hinson Collection.

University of Georgia Library, Athens. Howell Cobb Collection; Cobb-Erwin-Lamar Collection; Telamon Cuyler Collection; Jones Collection.

Emory University Library, Atlanta. Willink Papers.

Georgia Historical Society Library, Savannah. William P. Brooks Papers.

Clemson University Library, Clemson. Pendleton 'Agricultural

Society Papers; John C. Calhoun Papers (the best Calhoun collection is in the South Caroliniana Library, Columbia).
Alabama Department of Archives and History, Montgomery. Colin J. McRae Papers.
University of Alabama Library, Tuscaloosa. Shelby Iron Company Papers.

PRINTED SOURCES AND AUTHORITIES

Alexander, E. P. *Military Memoirs of a Confederate.* Edited by T. H. Williams. Bloomington, Ind., 1962.
Andrews, E. F. *The Wartime Journal of a Georgia Girl, 1864–1865.* Covington, Ga., 1976.
The Annals of the War, Written by Leading Participants, North and South. Philadelphia, 1879.
Augustinus, Aurelius. *Opera Omnia,* in: Migne, J. P. *Patrologiae Cursus Completus.* Series Latina Prior, vols. 32–47. Parisii, 1841 ff.
Barbour, P. L., ed. *The Jamestown Voyages Under the First Charter, 1606–1609.* 2 vols. London, 1969.
Bartram, W. *Travels Through North and South Carolina, Georgia, East and West Florida, the Cherokee Country, the Extensive Territories of Muscogulges or Creeck Confederacy, and the Country of the Choctaws.* 1791. Reprint. Savannah, Ga., 1974.
Bassett, J. S. *The Southern Plantation Overseer As Revealed by His Letters.* Northampton, 1925.
Belo, J. *Memórias de um Senhor de Engenho.* Edited by G. Freyre and J. L. do Rego. Rio de Janeiro, 1948.
Benzoni, M. Girolamo. *La Historia del Mondo Nuovo di M. Girolamo Benzoni, Milanese.* 1572. New critical edition. Graz, Austria, 1962.
Bradford, W. *Of Plymouth Plantation, 1620–1647.* Edited by S. E. Morison. New York, 1952.
Buck, J. *Cleburne and His Command.* Jackson, Tenn., 1959.
Burlamaqui, F. L. C. *Memoria Analytica acerca do commercio d'escravos e acerca da escravidão domestica.* Rio de Janeiro, 1837.
Byrd, W. *The Writings of Colonel William Byrd of Westover.* Edited by J. S. Bassett. Garden City, N.Y., 1901.
Calhoun, J. C. *The Papers of John C. Calhoun.* Edited by R. L. Meriwether and W. A. Hemphill. 9 vols. to date. Columbia, S.C., 1959 ff.
Calmon du Pin e Almeida, M. *Ensaio sobre o Fabrico do Assucar.* Bahia, 1834.
Capers, H. D. *The Life and Times of C. G. Memminger.* Richmond, Va., 1893.

Castiglione, B. *Il libro del Cortegiano*. 1528. Edited by V. Cian. Reprint. Florence, 1894.

de Charlevoix, P. *Histoire et description générale de la Nouvelle France*. 3 vols. Paris, 1744.

Chesnut, M. B. *A Diary From Dixie*. Edited by B. A. Williams. Boston, 1949.

Clay, J. *Letters of Joseph Clay, Merchant of Savannah*. Savannah, Ga., 1913.

Columbus, C. *Scritti di Cristoforo Colombo*. Pubblicati e illustrati da Cesare De Lollis. 2 vols. Roma, 1894.

The Confederate States Almanac. 4 vols. Vicksburg, Miss., and Mobile, Ala., 1861 ff.

Conyngham, D. O. *Sherman's March Through the South*. New York, 1865.

Daniel, J. W., ed. *Life and Reminiscences of Jefferson Davis by Distinguished Men of His Time*. Baltimore, Md., 1890.

Davis, J. *Jefferson Davis, Constitutionalist, His Letters, Papers and Speeches*. Edited by D. Rowland. 10 vols. Jackson, Miss., 1923 ff.

————. *The Papers of Jefferson Davis*. Edited by H. McIntosh. 2 vols. to date. Baton Rouge, La., 1971 ff.

————. *The Rise and Fall of the Confederate Government*. Edited by B. I. Wiley. 2 vols. New York and London, 1958.

Dawson, S. M. *A Confederate Girl's Diary*. Edited by J. I. Robinson. Bloomington, Ind., 1960.

DeBow, J. D. B. *DeBow's Review*.

————. *The Industrial Resources of the Southern and Western States*. 3 vols. New Orleans, 1852 ff.

DeLeon, T. C. *Four Years in Rebel Capitals*. Edited by E. B. Long, New York, 1962.

Easterby, J. H., ed. *The South Carolina Rice Plantation As Revealed in the Papers of Robert F. W. Allston*. Chicago, 1945.

Eden, R. *The First Three English Books on America (?1511–1555 A.D.)*. Translated and compiled by Richard Eden from the writings and maps of Pietro Martire of Anghiera, Sebastian Münster, and Sebastian Cabot. Edited by E. Arber. Birmingham, England, 1885.

Fernández de Navarrete, M. *Coleccion de los Viajes y descubrimientos que hicieron por mar los Espanoles desde fines del siglo XV*. 74 vols. Madrid, 1825 ff.

Fernández de Oviedo, G. *Historia general y natural de las Indias, islas y tierra firme del Mar Oceano*. 5 vols. Madrid, 1959.

Fitzhugh, G. *Cannibals All! Or, Slaves Without Masters*. Richmond, Va., 1857.

————. *Sociology for the South, Or, the Failure of the Free Society*. Richmond, Va., 1854.

Ford, C. W. *A Cycle of Adams Letters.* 2 vols. Boston, 1920.

Fremantle, Lt. Col. *The Fremantle Diary, being the Journal of Lt. Col. Fremantle, Coldstream Guards, On His Three Months in the Southern States.* Edited by W. Lord. Boston, 1954.

Gordon, J. B. *Reminiscences of the Civil War.* New York, 1905.

Gorgas, J. *The Civil War Diary of Josiah Gorgas.* Edited by F. Vandiver. University, Ala., 1947.

Hakluyt, R. *Divers Voyages Touching the Discouerie of America.* 1582. Reprint. New York, 1966.

————. *The Principal Navigations, Voyages and Discoveries of the English Nation.* 1589. Edited by D. B. Quinn and R. A. Skelton. Reprint. 2 vols. London, 1965.

————. *The Original Writings and Correspondence of the Two Richard Hakluyts.* Edited by E. G. R. Taylor. Cambridge, England, 1935.

Harrisse, H. *Bibliotheca Americana Vetustissima.* New York, 1866.

Helper, H. R. *The Impending Crisis of the South: How to Meet It.* New York, 1857.

Howell, V. Davis. *Jefferson Davis, Ex-President of the Confederate States of America: A Memoir by His Wife.* 2 vols. New York, 1890.

Hulton, J. P., and Quinn, D. B., eds. *The American Drawings of John White.* 2 vols. London, 1964.

Huse, C. *The Supplies for the Confederate Army.* Boston, 1904.

Johnson, J. *The Defense of Charleston Harbor.* Charleston, S.C., 1890.

Johnson, R. U., and Buel, C. C., eds. *Battles and Leaders of the Civil War.* 4 vols. New York, 1887 ff.

Jones, J. B. *A Rebel War Clerk's Diary.* 2 vols. New York, 1958.

Journal of the Congress of the Confederate States of America, 1861–1865. 7 vols. Washington, D.C., 1904 ff.

Kean, R. G. H. *Inside the Confederate Government.* Edited by E. Younger. New York, 1957.

Kettell, T. P. *Southern Wealth and Northern Profits.* New York, 1860.

Laurens, H. *The Papers of Henry Laurens.* Edited by P. M. Hamer et al. 5 vols. to date. Columbia, S.C.

Lee, R. E. *The Wartime Papers of Robert E. Lee.* Edited by C. Dowdey and L. Manarin. Boston, 1961.

Lyman, T. *Meade Headquarters, 1863–1865: Letters of Colonel Theodore Lyman from the Wilderness to Appomattox.* Edited by G. R. Agassiz. Boston, 1912.

Machiavelli, N. *The Arte of Warre.* London, 1562.

————. *Tutte le Opere Storiche e Letterarie.* Edited by G. Mazzoni and M. Casella. Florence, 1929.

Marshall, C. *An Aide de Camp of Lee*. Edited by F. Maurice. Boston, 1927.

Martyr de Angleria, P. *Opera*. Introductio Dr. Erich Woldan. Graz, Austria, 1966.

———. *De Orbe Novo Petri Martyris Anglerii Mediolanensis, protonotarii, et Caroli Quinti senatoris, Decades Octo, diligenti temporum obseruatione, et vtilissimis annotationibus illustratae, suôque nitori restitutae, labore et industria Richardi Hakluyti Oxoniensis Angli. Additus est in vsum lectoris accuratus totius operis index*. This is the famed Hakluyt edition of Peter Martyr. The most modern critical edition is the *Opera* of 1966, listed above.

———. *The Decades of the Newe Worlde or West India, Written in the Latine tounge by Peter Martyr of Angleria and Translated into Englyshe by Richarde Eden*. London, 1555.

Mather, C. *Magnalia Christi Americana: Or, the Ecclesiastical History of New England*. Edited by T. Robbins. 2 vols. Hartford, Conn., 1853.

Myers, R. M., ed. *The Children of Pride: A True Story of Georgia and the Civil War*. New Haven, Conn., 1972.

Oakeshott, W. *The Queen and the Poet*. London, 1960. Includes many poems by Raleigh not collected in *The Poems of Sir Walter Raleigh* (A. M. C. Latham, ed.).

Official Records of the Union and Confederate Navies in the War of the Rebellion. 31 vols. Washington, D.C., 1894 ff.

Olmsted, F. L. *A Journey in the Back Country*. New York, 1860.

———. *A Journey in the Seaboard Slave States*. New York, 1856.

———. *A Journey through Texas*. New York, 1857.

Le Page du Pratz. *Histoire de la Louisianne*. 3 vols. Paris, 1758.

Papers of the Military Historical Society of Massachusetts. 13 vols. Boston, 1895 ff.

Percy, W. A. *Lanterns on the Levee: Recollections of a Planter's Son*. Baton Rouge, La., 1973.

Phillips, U. B., ed. "The Correspondence of Robert Toombs, Alexander Stephens and Howell Cobb." *Annual Report of the American Historical Association* II (1911).

Pinckney, E. L. *The Letterbook of Eliza Lucas Pinckney, 1739–1762*. Edited by E. Pinckney et al. Chapel Hill, N.C., 1972.

Pringle, R. *The Letterbook of Robert Pringle*. Edited by W. B. Edgar. 2 vols. Columbia, S.C., 1972.

Pryor, S. A. *Reminiscences of Peace and War*. New York, 1924.

Quinn, D. B., ed. *The Roanoke Voyages, 1584–1590*. 2 vols. London, 1955.

———, ed. *The Voyages and Colonizing Enterprises of Sir Humphrey Gilbert*. 2 vols. London, 1940.

————, and Cheshire, N. M., eds. *The New Found Land of Stephanus Parmenius.* Toronto, 1972.
Raccolta di Studi e Documenti pubblicati dalla Regia Commissione Colombiana nel Quarto Centenario della Scoperta dell'America. A cura di Cesare De Lollis. 2 vols. Roma, 1892.
Rains, G. W. *History of the Confederate Powder Works.* Augusta, Ga., 1882.
Raleigh, Sir W. *The Poems of Sir Walter Raleigh.* Edited by A. M. C. Latham. London, 1951.
Ramusio, G. B. *Delle Navigationi et Viaggi.* With an introduction by R. A. Skelton and an analysis of the contents by G. B. Parks. Amsterdam, 1970.
Richardson, J. D., ed. *A Compilation of the Messages and Papers of the Confederacy.* 2 vols. Nashville, Tenn., 1906.
de Rochefort, C. *Histoire Naturelle et Morale des Antilles de l'Amérique.* Rotterdam, 1658.
Roman, A. *The Military Operations of General Beauregard.* 2 vols. New York, 1883.
Ruffin, E. *The Diary of Edmund Ruffin.* Edited by W. K. Scarborough. 2 vols. Baton Rouge, La., 1971.
Russell, W. H. *My Diary North and South.* Boston, 1863.
Scharf, J. T. *History of the Confederate States Navy From its Organization to the Surrender of its Last Vessel.* New York, 1887.
Scheibert, J. C. *Seven Months in the Rebel States During the North American War, 1863.* Tuscaloosa, Ala., 1958.
Schwab, E. L., ed. *Travels in the Old South, Selected From Periodicals of the Times.* 2 vols. Lexington, Ky., 1973.
Smedes, S. D. *Memorial of a Southern Planter.* Edited by F. M. Green. New York, 1965.
Southern Historical Society Papers. 52 vols. Richmond, Va., 1876 ff.
Stone, K. *Brockenburn: The Journal of Kate Stone, 1861–1868.* Edited by J. Q. Anderson. Baton Rouge, La., 1955.
Strachey, W. *The Historie of Trauaile into Virginia Brittania.* Edited by R. H. Major. London, 1849.
Taylor, T. E. *Running the Blockade.* London, 1896.
du Tertre, J. B. *Histoire générale des Antilles habitées par les François.* 4 vols. Paris, 1667 ff.
Upton, E. *The Military Policy of the United States.* Washington, D.C., 1912.
The War of the Rebellion: A Compilation of the Official Records of the Union and Confederate Armies. 70 vols. Washington, D.C., 1880 ff.
Wilkinson, J. *The Narrative of a Blockade Runner.* New York, 1877.
Williamson, J. A., ed. *The Cabot Voyages And Bristol Discovery*

Under Henry VII. Cambridge, England, 1962. The original manuscript documents are in the Archivo di Stato, Milan, Italy.

Wise, J. S. *The End of an Era*. Boston, 1900.

Wroth, L. C., ed. *The Voyages of Giovanni da Verrazzano*. New Haven, Conn., and London, 1970.

Zubillaga, F., ed. *Monumenta Antiquae Floridae, 1566–1572*. Roma, 1946.

SECONDARY WORKS

Abernethy, T. P. *The South in the New Nation, 1789–1815*. Baton Rouge, La., 1961.

Alden, J. R. *The South in the Revolution, 1763–1789*. Baton Rouge, La., 1957.

Almagia', R. *L'importanza geografica delle navigazioni di Giovanni da Verrazzano*. Florence, 1962.

Amlund, C. A. *Federalism in the Southern Confederacy*. Chapel Hill, N.C., 1963.

Anderson, B. *By Sea and By River: the Naval History of the Civil War*. New York, 1962.

Andreano, R., ed. *The Economic Impact of the American Civil War*. Cambridge, Mass., 1962.

Armes, E. *The Story of Coal and Iron in Alabama*. Birmingham, Ala., 1910.

Bailor, K. M. "John Taylor of Caroline." *Virginia Magazine of History and Biography*, July 1967.

Bannon, J. *Bolton and the Spanish Borderlands*. Norman, Okla., 1964.

Barney, W. *The Road to Secession*. New York, 1972.

Barrett, J. G. *Civil War in North Carolina*. Chapel Hill, N.C., 1963.

Baxter, J. P. *The Introduction of the Ironclad Warship*. Cambridge, Mass., 1933.

Bearss, E. C. *Decision in Mississippi*. Jackson, Miss., 1962.

Bercovitch, S. *The Puritan Origins of the American Self*. New Haven, Conn., and London, 1975.

Berlin, I. *Slaves Without Masters*. New York, 1975.

Bernath, S. L. *Squall Across the Atlantic*. Los Angeles, 1970.

Bilodeau, R., et al. *Histoire des Canadas*. Montréal, 1971.

Black, R. C. *The Railroads of the Confederacy*. Chapel Hill, N.C., 1952.

Blassingame, J. W. *The Slave Community*. New York, 1972.

de Bloch, J. *La Guerre*. Paris, 1898 ff. 6 vols. New edition edited by S. E. Cooper. New York and London, 1973.

Bolton, H. E. *Coronado*. Albuquerque, N.Mex., 1949.

———. *The Spanish Borderlands*. New Haven, Conn., 1921.

Bonazzi, T. *Il sacro esperimento*. Bologna, 1972.

Boxer, C. R. *The Dutch in Brazil, 1624–1654*. Hamden, Conn., 1973.

———. *The Dutch Seaborne Empire, 1600–1800*. London, 1965.

———. *The Golden Age of Brazil, 1695–1750*. Berkeley, Calif., 1962.

———. *The Portuguese Seaborne Empire, 1415–1825*. London, 1969.

———. *Salvador de Sa and the Struggle for Brazil and Angola, 1602–1686*. London, 1975.

Brewer, J. H. *The Confederate Negro: Virginia's Craftsmen and Military Laborers*. Durham, N.C., 1969.

Bruce, K. *Virginia Iron Manufacture in the Slave Era*. New York, 1930.

Bruce, R. V. *Lincoln and the Tools of War*. Indianapolis, Ind., 1956.

Bryan, T. C. *Confederate Georgia*. Athens, Ga., 1953.

Burckhardt, J. *The Civilization of the Renaissance in Italy*. Edited by L. Goldscheider. London, 1950.

Calogeras, J. P. *Formacão Histórica do Brasil*. Rio de Janeiro, 1930.

Cappon, L. J. "Government and Private Industry in the Southern Confederacy." *Humanistic Studies in Honor of John Calvin Metcalf*. Charlottesville, Va., 1941.

Carpenter, J. T. *The South as a Conscious Minority, 1789–1861*. New York, 1930.

Case, L. M., and Spencer, W. F. *The United States and France: Civil War Diplomacy*. Philadelphia, 1970.

Cash, W. *The Mind of the South*. New York, 1921.

Catton, B. *The Coming Fury*. Garden City, N.Y., 1961.

———. *Never Call Retreat*. Garden City, N.Y., 1965.

———. *Terrible Swift Sword*. Garden City, N.Y., 1963.

Chandler, D. *The Campaigns of Napoleon*. New York, 1966.

Chiappelli, F., ed. *First Images of America*. 2 vols. Berkeley, Los Angeles, and London, 1976.

von Clausewitz, K. *Vom Kriege*. Bonn, 1966.

Coit, M. *John C. Calhoun: American Portrait*. Boston, 1950.

Coleman, K. *Colonial Georgia: A History*. New York, 1976.

———. *Confederate Athens*. Athens, Ga., 1968.

Collinson, P. *The Elizabethan Puritan Movement*. Los Angeles, 1967.

Connelly, T. L., and Jones, A. *The Politics of Command: Factions and Ideas in Confederate Strategy*. Baton Rouge, La., 1973.

Conrad, H. A., and Meyer, J. R. *The Economics of Slavery and*

Other Studies in Econometric History. Chicago, 1964.

Corley, F. F. *Confederate City: Augusta, Georgia and the Civil War.* Columbia, S.C., 1960.

Coulter, C. M. *College Life in the Old South.* New York, 1928.

Coulter, E. M. *The Confederate States of America, 1861–1865.* Baton Rouge, La., 1950.

———. *Wormsloe: Two Centuries of a Georgia Family.* Athens, Ga., 1955.

Crane, V. W. *The Southern Frontier, 1670–1732.*

Craven, A. O. *Edmund Ruffin, Southerner.* Baton Rouge, La., 1972.

———. *The Growth of Southern Nationalism, 1848–1861.* Baton Rouge, La., 1953.

———. *Soil Exhaustion as a Factor in the Agricultural History of Virginia and Maryland.* Urbana, Ill., 1926.

Craven, W. F. *The Southern Colonies in the Seventeenth Century, 1607–1689.* Baton Rouge, La., 1950.

———. *White, Red and Black.* Charlottesville, Va., 1971.

Dabney, V. *Virginia, the New Dominion.* Garden City, N.Y., 1971.

Davidson, B. *Africa: History of a Continent.* London, 1966.

———. *The African Genius: An Introduction to African Cultural and Social History.* Boston, 1969.

———. *Black Mother: The Years of the African Slave Trade.* Boston, 1961.

———. *A History of West Africa, 1000–1800.* London, 1967.

Davis, C. S. *Colin J. McRae: Confederate Financial Agent.* Tuscaloosa, Ala., 1961.

Davis, D. B. *The Problem of Slavery in the Age of the Revolution, 1770–1823.* Ithaca, N.Y., 1975.

———. *The Problem of Slavery in Western Culture.* Ithaca, N.Y., 1966.

Davis, R. B. *Intellectual Life in Jefferson's Virginia.* Chapel Hill, N.C., 1964.

Debien, G. *Plantations et esclaves à Saint-Domingue.* Dakar, 1962.

Degler, C. *Neither Black Nor White: Slavery and Race Relations in Brazil and the United States.* New York, 1971.

De Negri, T. O. *Storia di Genova.* Milano, 1968.

Dew, C. B. *Ironmaker to the Confederacy: Joseph R. Anderson and the Tredegar Iron Works.* New Haven, Conn., 1966.

Dodd, W. E. *The Cotton Kingdom.* New Haven, Conn., 1917.

Donald, D. *Charles Sumner and the Coming of the Civil War.* New York, 1961.

———. *Lincoln Reconsidered.* New York, 1961.

———, ed. *Why the North Won the Civil War.* New York, 1963.

Drewry, W. S. *Slave Insurrections in Virginia, 1830–1865.* New York, 1955.

Dunn, R. S. *Sugar and Slaves: The Rise of the Planter Class in the English West Indies, 1624–1713.* Chapel Hill, N.C., 1972.

Durden, R. F. *The Gray and the Black: The Confederate Debate on Emancipation.* Baton Rouge, La., 1972.

Earle, E. M., et al, eds. *Makers of Modern Strategy: Military Thought From Machiavelli to Hitler.* New York, 1967.

Eaton, C. *Freedom of Thought Struggle in the Old South.* New York, 1964.

———. *The Growth of Southern Civilization, 1790–1860.* New York, 1961.

———. *A History of the Old South.* New York, 1966.

———. *A History of the Southern Confederacy.* New York, 1954.

———. *The Mind of the Old South.* Baton Rouge, La., 1964.

———. *The Waning of the Old South Civilization.* Athens, Ga., 1958.

Eccles, W. J. *Canada Under Louis XIV, 1663–1701.* Toronto, 1964.

———. *The Canadian Frontier, 1534–1760.* New York, 1969.

———. *Canadian Society During the French Regime.* Montréal, 1968.

———. *France in America.* New York, 1972.

Elkins, S. M. *Slavery: A Problem in American Institutional and Intellectual Life.* Chicago, 1966.

Falls, C. *A Hundred Years of War.* London, 1954.

Fishwick, M. *Gentlemen of Virginia.* New York, 1960.

———. *Virginia: A New Look at the Old Dominion.* New York, 1959.

Fleming, W. L. *Civil War and Reconstruction in Alabama.* New York, 1905.

Fogel, R. W., and Engerman, S. L. *Time On the Cross: The Economics of Slavery.* 2 vols. Boston, 1974.

Foner, E. *Free Soil, Free Labor, Free Men: The Ideology of the Republican Party Before the Civil War.* New York, 1970.

Foster, S. *Their Solitary Way: The Puritan Social Ethic in the First Century of Settlement in New England.* New Haven, Conn., 1971.

Franklin, J. H. *From Slavery to Freedom.* New York, 1947.

Frégault, G. *Le XVIII siècle canadien.* Montréal, 1968.

———. *La civilisation de la Nouvelle France, 1713–1744.* Montréal, 1944.

Freehling, W. W. *Prelude to Civil War: The Nullification Controversy in South Carolina, 1816–1834.* New York, 1966.

Freyre, G. *Interpretação do Brasil.* Rio de Janeiro, 1947.

———. *Introdução à Historia da Sociedade Patriarcal no Brasil. I. Casa Grande e Senzala—Formação da Familia Brasileira sob o Regime de Economia Patriarcal.* 2 vols. Rio de Janeiro e São Paulo, 1946.

II. *Sobrados e Mucambos—Decadencia do Patriarcado Rural e Desenvolvimento do Urbano.* 3 vols. Rio de Janeiro, 1951.
———. *O Mundo que o Português criou.* Rio de Janeiro, 1940.
Fuller, J. F. C. *Armament and History.* London, 1946.
———. *The Conduct of War, 1789–1961.* London, 1961.
———. *The Decisive Battles of the Western World and Their Influence Upon History.* 3 vols. London, 1954 ff.
———. *The Generalship of Ulysses Grant.* Bloomington, Ind., 1957.
———. *Grant and Lee: A Study in Personality and Generalship.* Bloomington, Ind., 1958.
———. *Memoirs of an Unconventional Soldier.* London, 1936.
Gadol, J. *Leon Battista Alberti, Universal Man of the Early Renaissance.* Chicago, 1969.
Gara, L. *The Liberty Line: The Legend of the Underground Railroad.* Lexington, Ky., 1961.
Genovese, E. D. *In Red and Black: Marxian Explorations in Southern and Afro-American History.* New York, 1971.
———. *The Political Economy of Slavery.* New York, 1965.
———. *Roll, Jordan, Roll: The World the Slaves Made.* New York, 1974.
———. *The World the Slaveholders Made.* New York, 1969.
———, ed. *Plantation, Town and Country.* Urbana, Ill., 1974.
———, ed. *The Slave Economies of the New World.* 2 vols. New York, 1973.
———, ed. with Foner, L. *Slavery in the New World.* Englewood Cliffs, N.J., 1969.
Giraud, M. *Histoire de la Louisianne Française.* 4 vols. to date. Paris, 1953 ff.
Gisler, A. *L'Esclavage aux Antilles Françaises (XVII–XIX siècle): Contribution au problème de l'esclavage.* Fribourg, Switzerland, 1965.
Goff, R. D. *Confederate Supply.* Durham, N.C., 1969.
Goldstein, T. "Geography in Fifteenth Century Florence." *Merchants and Scholars.* Edited by J. Parker. Minneapolis, Minn., 1965.
von der Goltz, C. *The Nation in Arms.* London, 1914.
Goveia, E. V. *Slave Society in the British Leeward Islands.* New Haven, Conn., 1965.
Gray, L. C. *A History of Agriculture in the Southern United States to 1865.* 2 vols. Washington, D.C., 1933.
Gutman, H. G. *The Black Family in Slavery and Freedom, 1750–1925.* New York, 1976.
Halleck, H. W. *Elements of Military Art and Science.* New York, 1863.

Harris, M. *Origin of the Land Tenure System in the United States.* Ames, Iowa, 1953.

Harris, R. C. *The Seigneurial System in Early Canada.* Quebec, 1966.

Harrisse, H. *The Discovery of North America: A Critical, Documentary, and Historic Investigation.* London and Paris, 1892. New edition, Amsterdam, 1961.

Henderson, G. F. R. *The Science of War.* London, 1910.

——. *The Civil War: A Soldier's View.* Edited by J. Luvaas. Chicago, 1958.

Hill, L. B. *Joseph Brown and the Confederacy.* Chapel Hill, N.C., 1939.

——. "State Socialism in the Confederate States of America." *Southern Sketches*, Series 1, no. 9. Charlottesville, Va., 1936.

Innis, H. A. *The Fur Trade in Canada.* Toronto, 1956.

Johns, J. E. *Florida During the Civil War.* Gainesville, Fla., 1963.

Johnson, L. H. *The Red River Campaign.* Baltimore, Md., 1958.

Johnston, A. A. *Virginia Railroads in the Civil War.* Chapel Hill, N.C., 1961.

Johnston, J. H. *Race Relations in Virginia and Miscegenation in the Old South, 1776–1860.* Amherst, Mass., 1970.

de Jomini, H. *Précis de l'art de la guerre ou nouveau tableau analytique des principes et combinaisons de la stratégie, de la grande tactique et de la politique militaire.* Edited by F. Lecomte. 2 vols. Paris, 1894. The new edition of Osnabruck, 1973, does not reproduce this one, but that of 1855. The Lecomte edition is therefore preferred as the most complete, including the exceedingly interesting—and scarcely known—comments of Jomini about the American Civil War.

Jones, A. *Confederate Strategy from Shiloh to Vicksburg.* Baton Rouge, La., 1961.

Jones, H. M. *O Strange New World. American Culture: The Formative Years.* New York, 1964.

Jones, W. D. *The Confederate Rams at Birkenhead.* Tuscaloosa, Ala., 1961.

Jordan, W. *White Over Black: American Attitudes Toward the Negro, 1550–1812.* Chapel Hill, N.C., 1968.

Jordan, W. T. "Agricultural Societies in Antebellum Alabama." *Alabama Review* IV: 4 (October 1951): 241.

——. "Plantation Medicine in the Old South." *Alabama Review* III: 2 (April 1950): 83.

Klein, H. S. *Slavery in the Americas: A Comparative Study of Virginia and Cuba.* Chicago, 1967.

Knapp, V. "William Phineas Browne, Business Man and Pioneer

Mine Operator of Alabama." *Alabama Review* III: 2 (April 1950): 108.

Knappen, M. M. *Tudor Puritanism*. Chicago, 1939.

Knight, F. W. *Slave Society in Cuba During the Nineteenth Century*. Madison, Wis., 1970.

Lanctot, G. *Histoire du Canada*. 3 vols. Montréal, 1960 ff.

Lane, A., ed. *The Debate Over Slavery: Stanley Elkins and His Critics*. Urbana, Ill., 1971.

Lanning, J. T. *The Spanish Missions of Georgia*. Chapel Hill, N.C., 1935.

Lee, C. R., Jr. *The Confederate Constitutions*. Chapel Hill, N.C., 1963.

Lefler, H. T., and Powell, W. S. *Colonial North Carolina: A History*. New York, 1973.

Lefranc, P. *Sir Walter Raleigh, écrivain, l'oeuvre et les idées*. Paris, 1968.

Leonard, I. A., ed. *The Spanish Approach to Pensacola, 1689–1693*. Albuquerque, N.Mex., 1939.

Lerner, E. M. "Inflation in the Confederacy, 1861–1865." *Studies in the Quantity Theory of Money*. Edited by M. Friedman. Chicago, 1956.

————. "Monetary and Fiscal Programs of the Confederate Government, 1861–1865." *Journal of Political Economy* LXII (1954): 506.

————. "Money, Prices and Wages in the Confederacy, 1861–1865." *Journal of Political Economy* LXIII (1955): 20.

Liddell-Hart, B. H. *The Decisive Wars of History: A Study in Strategy*. London, 1929.

————. *Memoirs*. 3 vols. London, 1965.

————. *Sherman: Soldier, Realist, American*. New York, 1958.

Long, E. B. *The Civil War Day by Day: An Almanac, 1861–1865*. Garden City, N.Y., 1971.

Lonn, E. *Salt As a Factor in the Confederacy*. New York, 1933.

Ludendorff, E. *Der Totale Krieg*. München, 1935.

————. *Kriegshetze und Völkermorden in den letzen 150 Jahren*. München, 1936.

Luraghi, R. "The Civil War and the Modernization of American Society—Social Structure and Industrial Revolution in the Old South Before and During the War." *Civil War History* XVIII: 3 (September 1972): 230.

————. *Gli Stati Uniti*. Torino, 1972.

————. *Storia della Guerra Civile Americana*. 4th edition. Torino, 1975.

McDermott, J. F., ed. *The French in the Mississippi Valley*. Urbana, Ill., 1965.

————, ed. *The Spanish in the Mississippi Valley, 1762–1804.* Urbana, Ill., 1974.

Mandle, J. R. *The Plantation Economy: Population and Economic Change in Guyana, 1838–1960.* Philadelphia, 1973.

Massey, M. E. *Ersatz in the Confederacy.* Columbia, S.C., 1952.

May, L. P. *Histoire économique de la Martinique, 1635–1763.* Paris, 1930.

May, R. E. *The Southern Dream of a Caribbean Empire, 1854–1861.* Baton Rouge, La., 1973.

Merril, J. M. *Battle Flags South: The Story of the Civil War Navies on Western Waters.* Rutherford, N.J., 1970.

Milby, E. *The Siege of Charleston, 1861–1865.* Columbia, S.C., 1970.

Miller, P. *From Colony to Province.* Cambridge, Mass., 1953.

————. *The New England Mind: The Seventeenth Century.* New York, 1939.

————. *Orthodoxy in Massachusetts, 1630–1650.* Cambridge, Mass., 1933.

Mims, S. L. *Clobert's West India Policy.* New Haven, Conn., 1912.

Mitchell, B. *William Gregg, Factory Master.* Chapel Hill, N.C., 1928.

Moore, A. B. *Conscription and Conflict in the Confederacy.* New York, 1924.

Moore, B. *Social Origins of Dictatorship and Democracy.* New York, 1966.

Montgomery, H. *Howell Cobb's Confederate Career.* Tuscaloosa, Ala., 1959.

Montross, L. *War Through the Ages.* New York, 1960.

Morison, S. E. *Admiral of the Ocean Sea: A Life of Christopher Columbus.* Boston, 1942.

————. *The European Discovery of America.* Vol. 1. New York, 1971.

Murga Saenz, V. *Juan Ponce de Leon.* San Juan, 1959.

Nash, G. B. *Red, White and Black.* Englewood Cliffs, N.J., 1974.

Nevins, A. *The Statesmanship of the Civil War.* New York, 1959.

Nichols, J. L. *Confederate Engineers.* Tuscaloosa, Ala., 1957.

Nickerson, H. *The Armed Horde, 1793–1939.* New York, 1942.

Niebor, H. J. *Slavery as an Industrial System: Ethnological Research.* New York, 1971.

Oates, S. B. *To Purge This Land With Blood: A Biography of John Brown.* New York, 1970.

Olschki, L. *Storia Letteraria delle scoperte geografiche.* Florence, 1936.

Owsley, F. L. *States' Rights in the Confederacy.* Gloucester, Mass., 1961.

Parks, G. B. *Richard Hakluyt and the English Voyages*. New York, 1928.

Parks, J. H. *General Edmund Kirby Smith, CSA*. Baton Rouge, La., 1954.

Parry, J. H. *The Spanish Seaborne Empire*. London, 1966.

Patrick, R. W. *Florida Under Five Flags*. Gainesville, Fla., 1960.

———. *Jefferson Davis and His Cabinet*. Baton Rouge, La., 1944.

Patterson, O. *The Sociology of Slavery: An Analysis of the Origins, Development and Structure of Negro Slave Society in Jamaica*. London, 1967.

Pearce, R. H. *Savagism and Civilization: A Study of the Indian and the American Mind*. Baltimore, Md., 1967.

Pease, J. H. "A Note on Patterns of Conspicuous Consumption Amongst Seaboard Planters." *Journal of Southern History* XXXV: 3 (August 1969).

Perry, M. F. *Infernal Machines: The Story of Confederate Submarine and Mine Warfare*. Baton Rouge, La., 1965.

Peytraud, L. *L'Esclavage aux Antilles Françaises avant 1789*. Paris, 1897.

Phillips, U. B. *The Course of the South to Secession*. New York, 1939.

———. *Life and Labor in the Old South*. Boston, 1929.

———. *The Slave Economy of the Old South*. Edited by E. D. Genovese. Baton Rouge, La., 1968.

———. *American Negro Slavery*. Edited by E. D. Genovese. Baton Rouge, La., 1973.

Potter, D. M. *The South and the Sectional Conflict*. Baton Rouge, La., 1968.

Powell, S. C. *Puritan Village: The Formation of a New England Town*. Middleton, Conn., 1963.

Pratt, E. A. *The Rise of Rail-Power in War and Conquest, 1833–1914*. London, 1915.

Quattlebaum, P. *The Land Called Chicora: The Carolinas Under Spanish Rule with French Intrusions, 1520–1670*. Gainesville, Fla., 1956.

Quinn, D. B. *England and the Discovery of America, 1481–1620*. New York, 1974.

———. *Raleigh and the British Empire*. London, 1974.

———, ed. *The Hakluyt Handbook*. 2 vols. London, 1974.

Ramsdell, C. W. *Behind the Lines in the Southern Confederacy*. Baton Rouge, La., 1944.

———. "The Control of Manufacturing by the Confederate Government." *The Mississippi Valley Historical Review* VIII (1931–1932): 231.

Randall, J. G., and Donald, D. *The Civil War and Reconstruction.* Boston, 1969.

Rawick, G. P. *The American Slave: A Composite Autobiography.* Westport, Conn., 1972.

Roland, C. P. *The Confederacy.* Chicago, 1960.

Romeo, R. *Le scoperte americane nella coscienza italiana del Cinquecento.* Milano e Napoli, 1954.

Ropes, J. C., and Livermore, W. L. *The Story of the Civil War.* 4 vols. New York and London, 1894 ff.

Ropp, T. *War in the Modern World.* New York, 1962.

Salone, E. *La Colonisation de la Nouvelle France.* Québec, 1916.

Scarborough, W. K. *The Overseer: Plantation Management in the Old South.* Baton Rouge, La., 1966.

Schwab, J. C. *The Confederate States of America, 1861–1865: A Financial and Industrial History.* New York, 1901.

Sereni, E. *Il capitalismo nelle campagne, 1860–1900.* Torino, 1947.

Sheridan, R. B. *Sugar and Slavery: An Economic History of the British West Indies, 1623–1775.* Baltimore, Md., 1972.

Simkins, F. B. and Roland, C. P. *A History of the South.* New York, 1972.

Simpson, A. *Puritanism in Old and New England.* Chicago, 1961.

Sirmans, M. E. *Colonial South Carolina: A Political History.* Chapel Hill, N.C., 1966.

Smith, A. E. *Colonists in Bondage: White Servitude and Convict Labor in America, 1607–1776.* Chapel Hill, N.C., 1947.

Smith, J. F. *Slavery and Plantation Growth in Antebellum Florida.* Gainesville, Fla., 1973.

Solís de Merás, G. *Pedro Menéndez de Avilés.* Gainesville, Fla., 1964.

Stampp, K. *The Peculiar Institution: Slavery in the Antebellum South.* New York, 1956.

Standard, B. W. *Columbus, Georgia in the Confederacy.* New York, 1954.

Starobin, R. *Industrial Slavery in the Old South.* New York, 1970.

Still, W. N. *Confederate Shipbuilding.* Athens, Ga., 1969.

———. *Iron Afloat: The Story of the Confederate Armorclads.* Nashville, Tenn., 1971.

Sydnor, C. S. *The Development of Southern Sectionalism, 1819–1848.* Baton Rouge, La., 1948.

Tannenbaum, F. *Slave and Citizen: The Negro in the Americas.* New York, 1947.

Taviani, P. E. *Cristoforo Colombo—La genesi della grande scoperta.* 2 vols. Novara, 1974.

Taylor, G. R. *The Transportation Revolution, 1815–1860.* New York, 1951.

Taylor, W. R. *Cavalier and Yankee: The Old South and the American National Character*. New York, 1961.

Thomas, E. M. *The American War and Peace, 1860–1877*. Englewood Cliffs, N.J., 1971.

———. *The Confederacy as a Revolutionary Experience*. Englewood Cliffs, N.J., 1971.

———. *The Confederate State of Richmond*. Austin, Tex., 1971.

Thompson, S. B. *Confederate Purchasing Operations Abroad*. Chapel Hill, N.C., 1935.

Todd, R. C. *Confederate Finance*. Athens, Ga., 1954.

Toplin, R. B., ed. *Slavery and Race Relations in Latin America*. Westport, Conn., 1974.

Trinkaus, E. *In One Image and Likeness: Humanity and Divinity in Italian Humanist Thought*. 2 vols. London, 1972.

Trudel, M. *The Beginnings of New France, 1524–1663*. Toronto, 1973.

———. *Les débuts du régime seigneurial*. Montréal, 1974.

———. *Montréal, la formation d'une société, 1642–1663*. Montréal, 1976.

———. *Histoire de la Nouvelle France*. 2 vols. to date. Montréal, 1963 ff.

———. *L'Esclavage au Canada Français*. Quebec, 1960.

———. *Le régime seigneurial*. Ottawa, 1966.

Tucker, G. *Zeb Vance, Champion of Personal Freedom*. Indianapolis, Ind., 1966.

Turner, G. E. *Victory Rode the Rails*. Indianapolis, Ind., 1953.

Vandiver, F. *Ploughshares Into Swords: Josiah Gorgas and Confederate Ordnance*. Austin, Tex., 1952.

———. "The Shelby Iron Company in the Civil War." *Alabama Review* I: 1–3 (January, April, July 1948).

———. *Their Tattered Flags: The Epics of the Confederacy*. New York, 1972.

Vicens-Vives, J., ed. *Historia Social y Económica de España y América*. 5 vols. Barcelona, 1957 ff.

Wade, R. C. *Slavery in the Cities: The South, 1820–1860*. New York, 1964.

Wertenbacker, T. J. *The Shaping of Colonial Virginia*. New York, 1958.

Wiley, B. I. *The Road to Appomattox*. Memphis, Tenn., 1956.

———. *Southern Negroes*. New Haven and London, 1965.

Williams, E. E. *Capitalism and Slavery*. New York, 1961.

Wiltse, C. M. *John C. Calhoun*. 3 vols. Indianapolis, Ind., 1944 ff.

Winters, J. D. *Civil War in Louisiana*. Baton Rouge, La., 1963.

Wood, P. H. *Black Majority: Negroes in Colonial South Carolina from 1670 through the Stono Rebellion*. New York, 1974.

Woodman, H. D. *King Cotton and His Retainers*. Lexington, Ky., 1968.

————, ed. *Slavery and the Southern Economy*. New York, 1966.

Woodward, C. V. *American Counterpoint: Slavery and Racism in the North-South Dialogue*. Boston, 1971.

————. *The Burden of Southern History*. New York, 1960.

Zavala, S. *De encomiendas y propriedad territorial en algunas regiones de la América Española*. Ciudad de Mexico, 1940.

Index

About the Author

Raimondo Luraghi was born and educated in Italy, receiving his Ph.D. degree in history from the University of Rome. In 1966 he wrote *Storia della Guerra Civile Americana* (A History of the American Civil War), which was awarded the Prize of the American Universities in Europe for the best book in American history written by a non-American and which some regard as the best one-volume history of the Civil War. Professor Luraghi teaches American history at the University of Genoa.